Understanding UK Defence Exports

This book offers a comprehensive overview of UK defence exports, as an example of the international trade in defence capabilities.

The work explores the subject of defence exports from the UK through various lenses, ranging from ethics, geopolitics, and national resilience to technology transfer, industrial partnering and military cooperation. By unveiling a multi-perspective model of defence exports, the book reveals the arms trade to be possessed of many meanings and understandings. At a moment in world history when the threat of state-on-state conflict has re-emerged, wedded to rapid technological changes in the practice of warfare, it is time to reassess the dynamics of the trade in arms through the experiences of the UK – a case study of defence exports from a mature democracy with a well-established military and defence industrial sector. Building upon extensive applied research across the UK defence environment, the work positions defence exports at the centre of a cat's cradle of multiple drivers and understandings, from the geopolitical to the commercial. Traditional and refreshed ethical arguments relating to the arms trade in the 21st century are also presented and explored which, together, reshape our knowledge and consideration of the roles of defence exports and the challenges that reside in its practice. With extensive access to ministers, policymakers, industrialists, campaigners and military commanders, the author is well-placed to deliver an appreciation of these multiple perspectives and explanations of defence exports, which are presented in an accessible manner for readers.

This book will be of much interest to students of defence and security studies, British politics and International Relations, as well as policymakers.

John Louth is a specialist adviser to the House of Commons Defence Select Committee. He is a co-author of British Defence in the 21st century (2019).

Routledge Advances in Defence Studies

Series editors:

Timothy Clack

University of Oxford, UK

Oliver Lewis

Rebellion Defence and *University of Southern California, USA*

Routledge Advances in Defence Studies is a multi-disciplinary series examining innovations, disruptions, counter-culture histories, and unconventional approaches to understanding contemporary forms, challenges, logics, frameworks, and technologies of national defence. This is the first series explicitly dedicated to examining the impact of radical change on national security and the construction of theoretical and imagined disruptions to existing structures, practices, and behaviours in the defence community of practice. The purpose of this series is to establish a first-class intellectual home for conceptually challenging and empirically authoritative studies that offer insight, clarity, and sustained focus.

Cultural Heritage in Modern Conflict
Past, Propaganda, Parade
Edited by Timothy Clack and Mark Dunkley

How Wars End
Theory and Practice
Edited by Richard Iron and Damien Kingsbury

Understanding UK Defence Exports
The International Trade in Defence Capabilities
John Louth

For more information about this series, please visit: https://www.routledge.com/Routledge-Advances-in-Defence-Studies/book-series/RAIDS

Understanding UK Defence Exports

The International Trade in Defence Capabilities

John Louth

Routledge
Taylor & Francis Group
LONDON AND NEW YORK

First published 2023
by Routledge
4 Park Square, Milton Park, Abingdon, Oxon OX14 4RN

and by Routledge
605 Third Avenue, New York, NY 10158

Routledge is an imprint of the Taylor & Francis Group, an informa business

British Library Cataloguing-in-Publication Data
A catalogue record for this book is available from the British Library

ISBN: 978-1-032-11778-2 (hbk)
ISBN: 978-1-032-11777-5 (pbk)
ISBN: 978-1-003-22149-4 (ebk)

DOI: 10.4324/9781003221494

Typeset in Times New Roman
by MPS Limited, Dehradun

Contents

About the Author

Professor Louth was in the military between 1987 and 2004 before turning his attention to commerce and academia. As an author, academic, and business leader, his passion is to explore, understand, and explain the complexities of defence capability generation and management drawn from a multi-faceted public–private enterprise, embracing defence prime contractors, technologists, SMEs, the armed forces, families, investors and governments.

Between 2011 and 2019, John was the director of the defence, industries, and society research programme at RUSI. He was also the Professor of Defence Management at the University of Roehampton Business School in London. John advised the Colombian government on defence industrial reform as part of the peace process, chaired the UK-Australian Defence Maritime Collaboration Dialogue in London and Sydney and was the independent chair of the MoD-Industry Nuclear Engineering Skills Review. Since 2012, John has been a specialist adviser to the UK House of Commons' Defence Select Committee. Before Brexit, he was the UK's representative to the EU on its annual defence capability review. He is a non-executive director and strategic adviser to a number of defence and advisory businesses and is a collaborating professor with the University of South Australia in Adelaide, where he is developing an Executive Defence MBA.

1 Introduction: The UK Trade in Arms: Exports – An End to Certainty?

Introduction

The UK trade in military weapons' systems is a complicated phenomenon, comprising multiple components, actors, opinions and contested understandings. One trivial illustration of this complexity is offered: over the years, the author has been welcomed into the boardrooms of hedge funds and banks in the City of London to analyse and discuss data-rich themes around British defence exports, principally to understand where the best corporate opportunities resided for the investor. In contrast, whilst attending a dinner of defence manufacturers, the author was spat at and verbally abused by campaigners objecting to the arms' trade and its fuelling, at the time, of the conflict in Yemen and the, understandably, perceived horrors of human suffering and waste associated with it. With the former experience, promoting UK defence exports was seen as a way to make money and contribute to national income and economic growth: in regard to the latter, it was perceived unequivocally that exported British weapons were causing the death and suffering of thousands and its practice was morally repugnant. These perspectives appear diametrically opposed yet a strong case could be made in favour of both analyses by researchers. Despite obvious differences in the emphasis placed on understanding, and possibly the positioning, values and stance of the inquisitor, defence exports exist in both spaces concurrently: one person's engine of growth and riches, whilst another's enabler of death and destruction.

There seems little doubt that the UK trade in arms has been championed as a key driver of national prosperity and socio-economic wellbeing from those in government and trade associations, especially as the economy recovers long-term post-Covid 19.[1] As part of this narrative, defence exports can be perceived as incubators of inward investment, employment opportunities, job security and skills' development, all of which contribute towards the health and wellbeing of local communities. In contrast, and emotively, such exports are seen often as components of a trade in death, destruction and key parts of a practice that can be deeply corrupt by practitioner design and government collusion or inaction and, through the capillary nature of the global defence trade, often further corrupting of those it touches.

DOI: 10.4324/9781003221494-1

This volume seeks to explore the phenomenon of defence exports from the United Kingdom through the multiplicity of understandings attached to it, in doing so testing the premise that government policies, corporate strategies and the legitimate challenges of campaigners combine to offer a comprehensive insight into the purposes, practices and outcomes of the trade, when contrasted against a partial understanding offered by a singular perspective located at an extreme. It is too glib to say that the voice of the activist seeking to ban completely the arms' trade somehow harmonizes with the defence business executive promoting her or his wares – they're singing different songs, after all. But one makes sense, resonates and can properly be heard only in the context of the other. So, to get a rounded and grounded understanding of UK defence exports, we have to explore the multiple narratives and explanations associated with it. That the phenomenon features so prominently in UK defence, economic and regional policies as well, as this volume will demonstrate, only adds to the importance of this undertaking.

The book, therefore, seeks to do two things:

- To collate, present, and analyse the multiple explanations of defence exports from the United Kingdom, presented as a national case study of the international trade in defence capabilities.
- To offer this commentary as a critical analysis of governmental policies and practices relating to defence and national security, prosperity, economics, global influence and high finance.

Building upon extensive, applied research across the UK defence environment, the author positions defence exports at the centre of a cat's cradle of multiple drivers and understandings, from the geopolitical to the commercial. Traditional and refreshed ethical arguments relating to the arms trade in the 21st century are clearly presented and explored which reshape our knowledge and consideration of the roles of defence exports and the challenges that reside in its practice.

This is a timely initiative. Global defence expenditure has grown markedly since the collapse of the Berlin Wall at the end of the 1980s. Based on a constant value of the US dollar, purchases of weapons and military support services have risen from $1.163 to $1.816 trillion in 2018, a rise of 56 percent. Part of that rise in defence spending can be explained by high-value military exports from countries such as the United Kingdom to emerging powers in the Middle East and Asia.[2] For example, in 2007, Saudi Arabia confirmed that it had signed an initial £4.43 billion contract with the United Kingdom and BAE Systems for 72 Typhoon aircraft. As a 'government-to-government' contract for highly regulated technology and equipment, the deal was constructed in effect to swap military equipment for oil with the UK government providing cash equivalents to the FTSE 100-listed BAE Systems. The contract was mired in allegations of corruption and executive privilege when the then Prime Minister, Tony Blair, and Attorney General Lord Goldsmith intervened to cancel a UK Serious Fraud Office investigation.[3] This prompts the critical question: is corruption in defence exports permitted by the state if conducted in the state's interests as defined by the state itself? How this sits comfortably, or not, with long-held notions of a parliamentary democracy, the separation of powers and the primacy of the rule of law are all themes explored by the book.

UK Defence Exports

UK defence exports is the general term given to the sale of UK-manufactured weapons, technologies, components and know-how to other countries around the world. As a practice, it can take multiple forms bounded by two extremes: a government-to-government export where the British government acts as broker, effectively purchasing the capabilities for onward sale to the receiving nation and, secondly, a direct sale from a private sector company in the United Kingdom to a foreign nation-state or company. In either case, the export contract is subject to governmental oversight and active approval through National Arms Export Licensing Criteria, though the effectiveness of export licensing is subject to debate.[4] There is little doubt, though, that the United Kingdom is a leading and active exporter of weapons-based capabilities, averaging second place in listings on a ten-year rolling basis, runner-up only to the United States. As such, Britain is Europe's leading Defence exporter[5] (Figure 1.1).

Top 10 Defence Exports by Nation, 2001-2010 ($ Bn)

USA	137.00
UK	95.00
Russia	53.00
France	41.00
Israel	18.00
Germany	16.00
Italy	14.00
Spain	12.00
Sweden	12.00
Canada	7.00

Figure 1.1 Defence Exports by Nation 2001–2010.

Source: *Financial Times* 1 February 2012.

Indeed, in the first decade of this century, between 2001 and 2010, global defence exports were as follows:

The UK's defence export value of $95 billion over this decade equalled the combined defence exports of France, Germany, Italy, Spain, and Sweden, an astonishing figure. The significance of Britain's 'excellence in defence exports – we're one of the best in the game,'[6] as one senior defence industrialist refers to it, and the UK government's policy commitment to its continuance, is explored in the following sections.

Multiple Understandings of Defence Exports

To seek a rounded, comprehensive understanding for the reader, approaches to the subject of UK Defence exports have been brigaded into a number of distinctive themes. These are presented in the following text.

Defence Exports as Ethical Imperatives

Within this theme, the subject of weapons' sales, and broader defence capabilities being traded from the United Kingdom, are explored through an ethical and moral framework. This analysis rests heavily on the critiques offered by campaigning organizations such as the Campaign Against the Arms Trade (CAAT)[7] and on think tanks like the Stockholm International Peace Research Institute (SIPRI).[8] The perspectives and understandings offered by this approach flow through alternative perspectives as they touch, or attempt to negate ethical considerations. Within the narrative, we especially consider ethical considerations through the twin lenses of corruption and the morality of providing lethal capabilities to autocracies and non-democratic monarchies, with the text especially focussed on Britain's involvement with the Middle East.

Defence Exports as Geopolitical Relations

This chapter will unravel UK policy relating to defence exports, placing the phenomenon within deliberate, geopolitical relationship management. Looking at how policy is considered and formed in No 10, the Cabinet Office, FCDO, and MoD, the chapter locates exports and defence sales as a traditional lever of state power within conventional understandings of international relations. The manner in which overt government policy directs and frames the strategies of UK-located defence prime contractors is considered along with notions of preferential treatment to these companies from the government, in terms of access to decision-makers and compliance or otherwise with specific defence export regulatory regimes. The protection by the government of these companies, from competition or legal obligation, for example, is also considered across the text.

Defence Exports as Economic Prosperity

The Strategic Defence and Security Review of 2010[9] introduced a new national security objective in that defence should promote national prosperity through its economic activities, especially those associated with exports. This is a major shift from the traditional purposes of expenditure on defence, namely to protect the homeland and project force overseas. This chapter introduces this policy stance and unpicks the government thinking behind it, which changes profoundly the traditional post-war political consensus relating to defence spending. The Dunne Report of 2018, which championed the contribution of defence to national prosperity, is considered and explored along with the impact, or otherwise, of economic activity for defence exports on the nations and regions of the United Kingdom. Through this changing governmental stance, defence exports are being positioned as economic and commercial imperatives, beyond traditional geopolitical explanations: a significant transformation from the post-war norm that provides a smart introduction into the following chapter.

Defence Exports as Business, Commerce, and Finance

Throughout the text, the business of defence exports is deconstructed into traditional practices of business development, sales, returns on investment into research and development and the growth in corporate turnover and expansion of an organization's balance sheet. In short, defence exports can be perceived as any other export, concerned with the expansion of, and profits from, international commerce. Regulation is driven by the lethality of the products under review – with the government overseeing merely a sensible and rational framework of permissions. Defence exports are shorn of the veneer of geopolitical rationalism and notions of a contribution to British national prosperity. Rather, exports are viewed as simply the manifestation of a company board's obligation to shareholders to maximize returns and the value within the business as a commercial going concern. The company's relationship with the government is revealed as one exploited to meet commercial targets and the drive for sales, which ministers and officials in government continually misunderstand and, consequently, often misrepresent.

Defence Exports as International Development

In contrast to the preceding characterization of UK defence exports as an overtly commercial phenomenon, this perspective locates the practice in the ongoing discourse of exports as assisting in the development of key allies – in this case, through the enhancement of their militaries and the promotion of skills and competencies across a nation's indigenous workforce. Within this narrative, defence exports are seen as a driver of the UK's self-stated obligations to other friendly nations through its commitment to international development. Significantly, through a careful analysis of public domain materials and interviews with FCDO (and ex-DFID) informants, the rationale of this practice is seen to pre-date overt policy stances on international aid associated with governments this century. This odd juxtaposition of the export of lethal equipment and know-how being seen, somehow, as a function of international aid is explored through a myriad of perspectives. Within this narrative, issues are explored around notions of national offset obligations between the United Kingdom and importing government and how such payments can be understood and critiqued.

Defence Exports as National Resilience

National resilience is now a championed concept within government and a common theme of ministers, commanders and industrialists when commenting on defence and security. Understandably but, perhaps, cynically, constructs such as defence exports are being repurposed and repackaged as events that contribute to UK national resilience. Proponents of this argument rest it on a number of key themes. First, that an appropriately skilled and competent workforce in the United Kingdom, that is adaptable, flexible, and rich in technological knowledge, is inherently resilient to exposure to societal shocks, issues, risks, and uncertainties. A surprising number of government policy statements make this point: an assertion of course, though highly rational, that can never be tested. Defence exports of modern technology-dependent equipment contribute towards the maintenance of such a workforce, located in specific regional hotspots, which can benefit from additional governmental and commercial research and development investment as necessary. Second, that defence jobs are typically high-end engineering, assembly and research roles that, over time, populate other sectors within the United Kingdom thereby growing resilience. Third, that defence businesses can adapt quickly in real time to defence operational challenges, such as those faced by the British military in Iraq, with this speedy flexibility being enabled by the market in defence exports. Put simply, without high-end defence exports, the United Kingdom would not have such a flexible workforce and would sacrifice potentially much of its inherent resilience. As a side issue, the tax associated with such sales and the corresponding retention of highly skilled jobs, benefits the country through corporation tax and income tax receipts, adding to resilience and wellbeing. This argument, whilst endemic in government, seems overblown, with the causality of assumptions imperious to test or critique. A broader macroeconomic analysis, data-led, is necessary.

Defence Exports as Technology Transfers

Defence equipment, components and technical know-how are, typically, protected technologies subject to national controls and secrecy legislation as well as being the intellectual property of the company or consortium in question. Its transfer, therefore, between countries as part of export contracts is a, supposedly, highly controlled and regulated business that is, in many ways, unique to the defence sector. A particular export control regime has emerged – and is being reformed still – to oversee these specific defence sectorial challenges. At the outset of this perspective, that notion of defence exceptionalism is challenged, given the significance of critical national infrastructure – utilities, health services, information technology and financial services, for instance – and the emerging national protections for these beyond the realms of defence equipment and services controls. As a consequence, this 21st-century complexity, associated with concepts of universality, connectivity and the Internet of Things, throws new light on practices of defence technology transfers that may well leave the UK weaker and more vulnerable as third parties benefit from critical capabilities developed and integrated in the United Kingdom. The manner in which the defence export regime is charged with addressing these sensitivities and potential fragilities is analysed and explored. This discussion is aligned to traditional corporate notions of intellectual ownership, value and the significance of intangible assets within a company's balance sheet. The challenge of government control over a financial value that is intrinsically private and commercial is unpacked, with boardroom informants increasingly uneasy with the reach of government into companies and the lockdown of their own commercial technologies as a 'national' good – to be held out of reach, perhaps, of the directors themselves. As such, the author tracks the histories and legacies of the agencies and offices associated with the control of defence exports as a regulated governmental activity, and the manner in which they have influenced the framework of regulation that exists today, which itself is explored and analysed. A significant element of this is the Parliamentary oversight of defence exports and its effectiveness, or otherwise, in contributing towards supposed democratic controls.

Defence Exports as Collaborative State-to-State and Government/ Industry Partnerships

In this analysis, defence exports are explored as examples of active partnerships between governments, private sector contractors, typically with extensive international supply chains, and user communities within the importing country. At the outset, the traditions of 'partnering' and partnerships across the defence ecosystem are defined and explored, with care taken to differentiate between legal terms and managerial practices. The text explores the different types and constructs of international collaboration, the prevalence of public–private partnerships and the role of government in championing these quasi-commercial constructs. The role of secrecy – state and commercial – and the significance of ownership of intellectual property is considered as part of this broader partnership debate. Lastly, the legitimizing narrative of partnering is explored, along with notions such as 'gainshare' and 'commercial best practice,' when it is seen that similar explanatory terms are offered by government and company executives to normalize defence contracts and relations, even when their legal and commercial constructs differ widely.

Defence Exports as Military Cooperation

The notion of wide-ranging complexity and modernist challenge brought forward from the preceding chapters is critiqued by the oldest and most simplistic explanation of defence exports from the United Kingdom to a friendly nation – namely, that it is merely a function of military-to-military cooperation. This explanation is promoted overtly by senior military informants in the United Kingdom, Middle East, and Australia, for example, where exports are seen as enablers of doctrinal alignment, common training and ways of working between militaries and the way for British military personnel to be embedded within a partner state's military forces. Historical examples of this are prevalent from the Napoleonic wars to the present day and form a dominant military explanation for the practice. Indeed, the Integrated Operating Concept, introduced by British generals in 2021, supported by the publication of the Integrated Review of defence and security in March,[10] heavily promotes military cooperation as a defence function for this century, reinforcing the importance of exports from the United Kingdom.

A Hybrid Challenge?

Mindful that legitimizing ideas of defence exports are embedded within modern defence doctrinal orthodoxy in the way stated above, what impact will this have on other understandings of this phenomenon and the manners in which a modern state and modern boardroom should exploit the opportunities and address the risks of defence technology transfer at the behest of commanders? This is the compelling challenge for both ministers and directors: the former as the United Kingdom seeks to meet its doctrinal aspirations, the latter as boardrooms navigate evermore demands on corporate governance and capital investment. This leads to very particular challenges of regulation and arms control which are explored throughout the text.

In the context of the defence policy stance of the United Kingdom, as evidenced by the Defence and Security Integrated Review (IR), the military command paper that followed it and the enveloping Defence and Security Industrial Strategy (DSIS),[11] particular focus is placed in the following chapters on commitments to exports through increasing government-to-government contracts, growth in national investment and the exploitation of commercial technological research for defence systems. These factors, in part, sit alongside governmental ambitions for defence exports to be levers of military capability and capacity building, at home and through

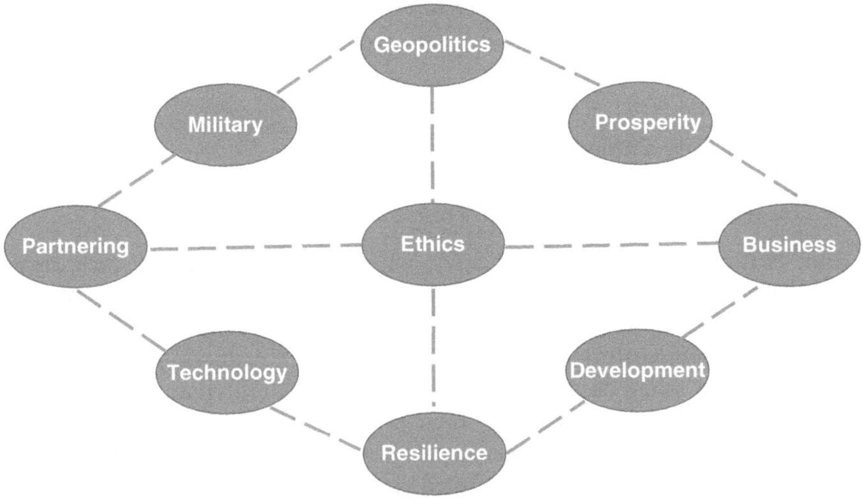

Figure 1.2 Multi-Perspective Model of Defence Exports.

Source: Author.

international partners – what could be perceived as an extension of the concept of 'global Britain.' Defence exports, therefore, could be conceptualized not simply as tools of political influence in political circles, but also as a function of British prestige.

These multiple understanding are configured into a multi-perspective model of defence exports which form the basis for each subsequent chapter of the book. Such a model allows, for the future, comparative analyses between the UK system of defence exports and those in other countries and jurisdictions. The model is captured as shown in Figure 1.2.

Approach

This approach is built upon the conceptual foundation that arms exports can be deconstructed into a number of distinctive, often contradictory, themes for review and dissection. The methodological approach is one of analysing these perspectives as a basis for drawing inferences, insights and understandings into normative claims and counter-claims across the defence export debate. To help with this, a significant literature review was undertaken: scholarly works, governmental policy statements, parliamentary and agency reports, as well as materials from arms trade campaigners and non-government organizations (NGOs). This desk-top review was complemented by structured and semi-structured interviews, the results of which are peppered throughout the text. Interviews were conducted on the condition of anonymity, except where indicated.

Also, the text leads heavily on certain UK-registered defence businesses from large, international prime contractors, through to niche, technology-rich small to medium-sized enterprises (SMEs). These companies will be unveiled throughout the text.

The British Government and Defence Exports

The Department for International Trade

Given Britain's perceived significance within the international arms trade, some scene-setting and introductory data sets seem appropriate. A good place to start is the UK's House of Commons, the staff of which uses very deliberate language to define defence exports as the export of military and dual-use items (that could be used for military or civilian use) to other nations.[12] The Department for International Trade is the government ministry responsible for overseeing this practice and gathering data on its execution and, indeed, two organizations within this department of state are to be found at the forefront of this undertaking. These are the Defence and Security Organization (DSO) and the Export Control Organization (ECO). The DSO, especially, collects data on UK defence exports by means of a periodic survey of UK defence companies based on orders received. From this data, the DSO calculates that over the past 35 years the average value of exports was £7.2 billion per annum whilst, when considering the last ten years, the average value of exports per annum was £8.9 billion, assuming a base year of 2018. The trajectory for defence exports is upwards.[13]

In 2018, the Middle Eastern states accounted for about 60 percent of UK defence exports, with North America consuming 18 percent of exports of defence materials. In contrast, Europe accounted for 11 percent of defence exports, the Asia-Pacific region 9 percent, with Africa and Latin America accounting for the remaining 2 percent, split evenly between the regions. The importance of the Arab states, especially Saudi Arabia, historically to UK defence exports will become increasingly clear through the course of this text. What will become obvious also is that these same states are the targets for future defence export campaigns from the United Kingdom. Britain is a leading armourer of the Arab autocracies and will be so for many years to come as a product of deliberate governmental and commercial strategies (Figure 1.3).

The DSO's sister organization within the Department for International Trade, the ECO, a little confusingly characterizes exports of defence materials as a trade in 'strategic goods.' Within this definition, these materials break down into three further categories:

- Military goods, such as aircraft, combat rifles, and warships;
- Civilian/non-military goods, for example, imaging equipment and data processors; and
- Dual-use goods, which are civilian goods being sold to a country for a specific military purpose.

Region	% Exports (Based on £ values)
Middle East	58
North America	17
Europe	15
Asia Pacific	8
Africa	1
Latin America	1

UK EXPORTS TO GLOBAL REGIONS: 2011-2020

Figure 1.3 UK Defence Exports by Region.

Source: Author.

Against these categories, the criteria for issuing an export licence is determined by four further factors:

- The nature of the goods to be exported;
- The destination of those goods and materials;
- The ultimate end user of materials; and
- The status of the trade activities of the goods being exported.

It is, in short, a complicated legal and bureaucratic set of processes between government officials and industrial executives, often subject to lobbying by special interest groups, advocates from public relations firms and the receiving country's ambassador in London. By way of introduction, for now, it is sufficient to note that, in 2019, just over 10,200 licences were issued for Standard Individual Export Licences (SIEL) at a total export value of £8.7billion, an increase in almost a quarter from 2008.[14]

It should be noted also that, whilst the DIT is the government department with responsibility for the issue of export licences and for overseeing the integrity of export controls, British defence exports are calibrated by decision-making in No 10 Downing Street, the Cabinet Office, the Treasury and elsewhere in government – especially the MoD. Successful defence exports from the United Kingdom seem to occur when a particular capability is in service with the UK armed forces. Quite often, therefore, as part of an overseas' sales campaign, the British military overtly champion equipment that they use to fellow soldiers, sailors and airmen and women in the target country. As one senior UK MoD official described it:[15]

> The Prime Ministers fingerprints are over all major defence exports. The MoD is used to drive the deal with its soldiers as salesmen; DIT just keep the records.

Economic Prosperity

If, as stated earlier, that prime ministers like to be associated with defence exports, this is probably due to two distinct reasons. The first is that national leaders like to be seen with the British military and the defence equipment they use. From Mrs Thatcher astride a British tank to Mr Blair sipping tea in Iraq, prime ministers enjoy the prestige of military contact. More importantly, perhaps, is the sense that defence exports drive economic benefits to the United Kingdom and indicators of a commitment to prosperity or national earnings are catnip to the political classes.

In 2018, Philip Dunne MP, an ex-Minister for defence procurement, was asked by the Secretary of State for Defence to produce a report on the UK Defence contribution to prosperity. His extensive review articulates clearly the duality of military and economic benefits:[16]

> Defence makes possible our secure domestic environment and rules-based international order so that we can live and prosper, protected from the devastation of war and the impact of terrorism … It protects the trade routes that carry the goods we consume. It guards the underwater cables and satellites that convey the communications that connect us with other nations. It counters the cyber-attacks that could bring our technologically-dependent lives to a standstill. Virtually invisible, this protection underpins our economic growth.
>
> Defence's direct contribution to GDP includes over £7 billion of exports generated on average each year in addition to the MoD budget of £37 billion. Defence's role as a customer and industrial partner with high growth sectors in the economy generates more growth, notably in the aerospace, engineering, space, cyber and now the knowledge and creative sectors. It is hard to quantify. But it is very valuable, both in the ability of the Armed Forces to deploy successfully and to keep the UK ahead of its competitors and adversaries in the future.

Region or Nation	MoD Expenditure with Industry (£M)	Jobs supported by MoD expenditure with Industry
Scotland	1,600	10,500
Northern Ireland	103	600
Wales	945	6,300
North West England	2,000	12,300
North East England	100	700
Yorkshire and Humberside	232	1,800
East Midlands	845	6,900
West Midlands	918	4,700
East of England	918	5,700
London	568	7,100
South East England	4,900	33,100
South West England	5,100	33,500

Figure 1.4 UK Defence Prosperity Data.

Source: The Dunne Report 2018.

For Dunne, the driver of this twin purpose of security and growth would be the recognition in government that prosperity was an enduring and explicit objective for Defence. The MoD, in particular, needed to prioritize and incentivize exports, necessarily becoming increasingly agile in its procurement practices. Given that national prosperity, as policy, is so critical, the table below articulates the Defence contribution to notions of economic benefit and growth across the nations and regions of the United Kingdom (Figure 1.4).

A quick glance at the data reveals, of course, that prosperity through the 'Defence Pound' is far from evenly distributed across the United Kingdom. Whilst the southwest of England, for example, benefits from an employment figure of over 33,000 people and receives £5.1 billion in income from the MOD, Northern Ireland, in contrast, receives only £100 million or so and generates merely 600 jobs. Whilst there are historical reasons for these figures, with a large aerospace design and engineering hub located in Bristol, for instance, how this situation sits easily with political ideas of 'levelling up' and an economic commitment for growth pan-UK will be considered in subsequent chapters. For now, it is sufficient to note that 'prosperity,' 'defence exports,' and 'MoD expenditure' are linked concepts in the minds of decision-makers. Moreover, British Defence has a split personality of security and prosperity that can prove hard to reconcile across the policy sphere, as the reader shall come to see.

Defence Exports and Government Orthodoxy

Defence exports from a nation to a client-state result from deliberate government policy. In the case of the United Kingdom, the British government published its integrated review[17] of defence, security, international development and foreign policy in March 2021, tagged as the largest and most strategic review of the UK's defensive posture since the end of the Cold War. As the guiding policy paper to take Britain into the 2030s and beyond, the vision for 'Global Britain' could be summarized as follows:

- The United Kingdom was poised to take a more active part in sustaining and protecting the international order in which democracies flourish, working together to protect human rights and international norms of trade and exchange.
- Prosperity would be championed through innovation in science and technologies that would both boost national income and strategic advantage.
- As a maritime trading nation, the United Kingdom would champion free trade and commit forces to ensure that trading routes remain open and navigable.
- The main instruments of hard power, the armed forces and the intelligence and security agencies, along with the diplomatic service, would be transformed into the most effective and innovative organizations when compared to global peers, developing a critical national space programme and becoming one of the world's leading democratic cyber powers.[18]

The bulk of the UK's security focus would be on the Euro-Atlantic region, with NATO as the foundation of collective security in this geographical area. Russia was recognized as the biggest threat to the security of this region though, significantly, the policy review also talked of a tilt to the indo-pacific, conscious that by the 2030s, geopolitical and economic centres of gravity would have migrated significantly east of Europe. In this regard, China would continue to become increasingly assertive and powerful on the global stage, posing the biggest state-based threat to the UK's economic security. Accordingly, China-facing capabilities were to be the subject of investment, including changes to the UK force structure and capabilities focussed in the Indo-Pacific region.

It is significant to note that words such as 'prosperity' and 'economic security' were very much part of the fabric of a policy review focussed on defence and security strategy. Indeed, senior figures in government and the military were happy to brief privately that defence exports, being championed from London, were a significant component of this thinking. This was overtly expressed in the Defence and Security Industrial Strategy (DSIS), a companion document to the IR, once more published in March 2021.[19]

Key elements of the DSIS comprised a commitment for at least £6.6 billion in defence research and development funding and, in a reference to Dunne, the commitment by the government was made to produce a new science and technology strategy. There was a further agreement to produce a new SME action plan to reinvigorate the relationship with smaller, supposedly more innovative design, technology and engineering businesses. Even more strategies were set to flow: a land sector strategy; an intellectual property strategy; a defence supply chain innovation strategy; and a bespoke acquisition strategy for the newly formed Defence Centre for Artificial Intelligence.[20] Moreover, the DSIS stated that there were to be a range of distinctive 'protected segments' of defence which were to be protected from overseas' ownership and interference, these being:

- Strategic nuclear capabilities;
- Offensive cyber;
- Crypt key intelligence capabilities;
- Complex weapons;
- Novel weapons;
- Test and evaluation capabilities; and
- Chemical, biological, radiological, and nuclear protective and offensive capabilities.

We shall return to these strategic documents later in the book but defence exports, in the 2020s and beyond, were to be undertaken through a cat's cradle of emerging governmental policies and strategies linked to notions of prosperity, security and specific, sectorial reform. How this was to impact decision-making in boardrooms and between investors was paid scant attention by policymakers.

Defence Exports and Charges of Corruption

There are many notable works – some scholarly, others glib and emotive – that paint a picture of an out-of-control global arms trade. This seems to be for many citizens a compelling and enduring characterization and there is, of course, some historical legitimacy attached to this perspective. In 2011, for example, Andrew Feinstein published an account of the Al Yamamah deal between the UK Government, Saudi Arabia, and BAE Systems that commenced with Feinstein's description of Prince Bandar bin Sultan bin Abdul Aziz Al-Saud, Saudi Arabia's ambassador to Washington, arriving at Crawford, Texas in 2002. He alighted from his private Airbus jet to lobby US President George W. Bush to go to war the following year against Iraq.[21]

> The £75m Airbus … was a gift from the British arms company BAE Systems. It was a token of gratitude for the Prince's role, as son of the country's Defence Minister, in the biggest arms deal the world has seen. The Al Yamamah – 'the dove' – deal signed between the United Kingdom and Saudi Arabia in 1985 was worth over £40bn. It was also arguably the most corrupt transaction in trading history. Over £1bn was

paid into accounts controlled by Bandar. The Airbus – maintained and operated by BAE at least until 2007 – was a little extra, presented to Bandar on his birthday in 1988.

Campaigners and certain academics argue that not only is the trade in weapons morally repugnant and institutionally corrupt – as presented by the payments to Prince Bandar, for instance – but also that the economic benefits of such deals are overstated. Such campaigners point to defence companies funding of Public Relations agencies, think tanks and university departments to make the economic case on their behalf. They argue that the UK Exchequer receipts from companies and employees of the arms companies are exaggerated and that, in any case, such jobs are dependent upon public sector sponsorship that could provide more employment opportunities if spent on alternative sectors to defence.

The book will explore these charges of corruption, inappropriate influence and manipulation of public discourse. But it is important to note that any discussion on defence exports, to be effective, must accept that charges of corruption permeate the public narrative. Part of this narrative, of course, envelopes senior political figures, boardroom directors and executives from massive publicly-listed companies and influential supposed 'thought leaders' from universities and London think tanks. The perspective that arms companies somehow shape the popular discourse, paradoxically to counter the insights of anti-arms trade campaigners, seems pervasive – the legitimacy or otherwise of this view are themes that weave through this work.

Structure of the Book

Based on the author's multi-perspective model of defence exports, the book is structured as follows:

- Chapter 1: Introduction: the UK trade in arms and exports – an end to certainty?
- Chapter 2: Defence exports as ethics;
- Chapter 3: Defence exports as geopolitical relations;
- Chapter 4: Defence exports as economic prosperity;
- Chapter 5: Defence exports as business, commerce, and finance;
- Chapter 6: Defence exports as international development;
- Chapter 7: Defence exports as national resilience;
- Chapter 8: Defence exports as technology transfer;
- Chapter 9: Defence exports as partnerships;
- Chapter 10: Defence exports as military cooperation;
- Chapter 11: Conclusion – towards a new understanding.

Chapters 2–10, taken as one, provide a strong argument for there being multiple meanings of, and reasons for, defence exports that are valuable together in forging a richer, more coherent and inclusive understanding of this key governmental and commercial phenomenon. Chapter 11, by way of conclusion, reframes the core themes from this analysis into an explanatory model of defence exports that offers policymakers, regulators, analysts, and citizens an effective roadmap for developing and critically assessing the institutions, personnel, processes and practices of the UK trade in defence capabilities.

At the start of each chapter, a summary box takes the reader through the core themes that are to be encountered so that the principal understandings to be gleaned from the chapter are flagged to the reader ahead of an engagement with the text.

An appendix at the end of the book offers key statistics and a data set relating to UK defence exports. It considers both UK trends and seeks to place British defence exports within an international, comparative context.

Conclusion

This chapter has introduced the reader to notions of modern defence sales from the UK that are multiple and contested. These differences in understanding and conflicted perspectives have been brought together into a Multi-Perspective Model of Defence Exports, with this forming the basis of each subsequent chapter in the book. In this manner, defence exports are deconstructed into accessible constituent components, ripe for analysis. Laying out the phenomenon in such a way also makes clear that defence exports touch on major governmental and societal themes: for instance, security, prosperity, influence, commerce, resilience, identity, value and values, to name but a few. Could it be that an exploration of defence exports is also an enquiry into the nature of ideas relating to nationhood, civilization and citizenship? The following pages may reveal more than we anticipate, perhaps even something of ourselves in this moment of strategic change.[22]

Notes

1 https://www.nottingham.ac.uk/vision/vision-economy-after-covid-19
2 Andrew T.H. Tan (ED), Res*earch Handbook on the Arms Trade* (Cheltenham: Edward Elgar Publishing, 2020).
3 Andrew Feinstein, *The Shadow Word: Inside the Global Arms Trade* (London: Hamish Hamilton, 2011) p. 129.
4 K. Wright, *Arms Control and Security: The Changing Role of Conventional Arms Control in Europe* (London: Ashgate, 2000).
5 Jon Stone, 'Britain is now the second biggest arms dealer in the world,' *The Independent* (London, 5 September 2016).
6 Michael Formosa, Managing Partner of Renaissance Strategic Advisors, speaking with the author on 19th July 2022.
7 https://caat.org.uk
8 https://www.sipri.org

9 HM Government, *Securing Britain in an Age of Uncertainty: The Strategic Defence and Security Review* (London: The Stationery Office, 2010).
10 HM Government, *Global Britain in a competitive age: The Integrated Review of Security, Defence, Development and Foreign Policy* (London: The Stationery Office, 2021).
11 HM Government, *Defence and Security Industrial Strategy* (London: The Stationery Office 2021).
12 House of Commons Library, UK Arms Exports Statistics, 1 December 2021. https://researchbriefings.files.parliament.uk/documents/CBP-8310.pdf
13 *Ibid.*
14 *Ibid.*
15 Official speaking to the author in confidence in London on Friday 12 November 2021.
16 Philip Dunne MP, *Growing the Contribution of Defence to UK Prosperity: A Report for the Secretary of State for Defence*, (London: July 2018) p. 5.
17 HM Government, *Global Britain in a competitive age*
18 Claire Mills and Louisa Brooke-Holland, *House of Commons Briefing Paper: Integrated Review 2021* (London: House of Commons Briefing Paper No. 9171, 17 March 2021).
19 HM Government, *Defence and Security Industrial Strategy*
20 At the time of writing in 2022, these strategies to date have not emerged from government.
21 Andrew Feinstein, p. xvii.
22 Michael Clarke, *The Challenge of Defending Britain* (Manchester: Manchester University Press, 2019).

2 Defence Exports and Ethics

Introduction

For an element of general society, the concept of defence exports is tarnished by stories of corruption, wrong-doing and slaughters of the innocent.[1] Authors such as Andrew Feinstein have sought to portray the global arms trade as a chilling, heart-breaking shadow world of actors that play by their own rules and codes of practice, immune to oversight, investigation, and the rule of law.[2] Politicians and government officials are said to collude with sellers to side-step proper scrutiny of defence exports, citing the national interest or desire for increased national prosperity.[3]

> The corrupt and secretive way the industry operates undermines accountable democracy in both buying and selling countries. The arms trade accounts for over 40 per cent of corruption in all world trade. The combination of the sheer magnitude of the contracts, the very small number of people who make the purchasing decisions and the cloak of national security lends itself to bribery and corruption on a massive scale.

Campaigners, such as those associated with the Campaign Against the Arms Trade (CAAT), contribute to this narrative of corruption and unlawful practices, but also point to the ethics of the trade. How can it be right, they might say, that undemocratic, autocracies in the Middle East can buy sophisticated weapons and munitions from the UK to use, potentially, indiscriminately on the populations of the Yemen, for example? Does the UK's overt contribution to the immense suffering in Yemen, through defence exports, render the British state and UK-registered defence businesses involved in this trade deeply immoral?

This chapter makes the case for defence exports to be viewed through the twin and interconnected lenses of morality and corruption. It suggests that questions of 'right' and legality are corralled within a system that has favoured, historically, bad practices over good, motivated by multiple drivers. This system, itself, of course, does not just embrace the purchasing country and the UK-registered defence business, but the British state and the laws

DOI: 10.4324/9781003221494-2

and conventions associated with a mature democracy. In this manner, defence exports are perceived as a possible cancer at the centre of British politics and commerce, fatally weakening institutions and individuals alike.[4] For many, it represents the dominant discourse of an understanding of defence exports from the United Kingdom, with all other perspectives and arguments paling in the shade of this narrative.

The narrative itself is explored in the pages below through the eyes, initially, of academics working in this area of research and, thereafter, the campaigners who reject outright the British trade in arms exports. The chapter begins with a sense of the stories told of corruption in defence sales and concludes with a charge sheet, from campaigners, that could be levelled at the whole of the United Kingdom.

Corruption: The Stories Told: An Example

Following the release from prison of Nelson Mandela in February 1990, South Africa underwent an unparalleled programme of state-building and reconciliation between ethnic groups and attempted to embrace the principles and practices of a modern democracy.[5] It was for many around the world a set of events where ideas of tolerance, forgiveness and the promise of pluralist statehood brought hope. At the end of the 20th century, and as is the case still it seems, the country was riddled with huge socio-economic issues of unemployment, appalling housing conditions, violence, and a health emergency driven by the Aids catastrophe that, in South Africa, ran into millions of victims.

With the end of apartheid and the birth of the 'Rainbow Nation,' there was an expectation that a government led by the African National Congress (ANC) would reduce defence spending in favour of health and infrastructure projects. In 1999, however, the South African Government, under Thabo Mbeki, announced a major procurement of defence items: training and fighter aircraft from the UK and Sweden; frigates and other maritime assets from Germany, and helicopters to be purchased from Italy. The cost of these defence imports would total over US$6 billion.

In response to this, the country's Auditor General furnished a report to the relatively new constitutional body of the Public Accounts Committee that appeared to provide evidence of malpractice in the procurement and clear commercial untruths being provided by vendors to South African competition authorities:[6]

> The procurements, known collectively as the "arms deal," were wracked by allegations of corruption from the start … About $300 million was paid in commissions and bribes to middlemen, senior politicians, officials, their associates and the ANC itself. The bribes were a key motivation in the deal, especially the need to finance the party and upcoming elections.

About 50 percent of the deal was related to fighter jets: Hawk aircraft from BAE Systems in the UK and Gripen aircraft from Saab, headquartered in Sweden. It seems, however, that the South African Air Force commanders wanted neither and had other, cheaper, preferences which were not procured despite acquisition principles of open competition and objective bid assessment processes.[7]

Instead, the BAE Systems/Saab offset deal, actively promoted to the South Africans by both British and Swedish governments, secured competition victory. Offsets, or countertrade, programmes are those where the supplier business commits to invest in the industry or society of a purchasing state, thereby 'offsetting' the costs of the transaction. Such arrangements are controversial, and the World Trade Organisation has banned their use as a contract evaluation tool in all international trade deals other than those associated with defence. According to the work of the South African Public Accounts Committee, through the lobbying principally of the UK Government and British industry:[8]

> South Africa had been taken for a ride. The arms companies had persuaded political leaders and military officials that they needed far more equipment than had originally been envisaged. They charged a premium, in one instance 35 percent more than others paid for the same equipment and promised unrealized economic benefits from the contracts. There was immediately clear evidence of conflicts of interest and possible corruption.

This tale of misspelling and misrepresentation, coupled with alleged acts of bribery and corrupt practices, is but one of many supposed examples of UK defence exports in action offered by campaigners. The teller might even assert that the absence of convictions and legal jeopardy points to direct political influence having been exercised over investigative bodies and charging authorities. Illegal practices, active political bias, and commercial bad practice, in stories such as this, seem engrained and institutionalised, with the principal motivation being financial gain for importing businesses, individuals, and even political parties.

Similar stories will be unpacked in the following chapters as we seek a richer, more nuanced and less binary understanding of UK defence exports. For now, though, we turn to capturing current and emerging academic understandings of the potential for corruption in the arms trade.

Defence Exports and Ethics: The Academic Case

At an international level, global defence spending has risen in real terms since the end of the Cold War at the end of the 1980s. This is surprising, in many ways, as the collapse of the Soviet Union and its empire in Eastern Europe, combined with the global financial shocks of 2008, for some analysts, suggest that a peace dividend should have been generated suppressing defence spending. Nonetheless:[9]

> ... total world defence spending measured in constant 2018 prices rose from US$1,516 billion in 1989 at the end of the Cold War, to US$1,914 billion in 2019 ... Some regions have seen a dramatic increase in defence spending since 1989. Indeed, spending in Asia/Oceania rose from US $143 billion in 1989 to US$531 billion in 2019 ... [The] Middle East also saw an increased, from US$68.6 billion in 1989 to US$ 181 billion.[10]

Certain academics would ascribe the following *drivers* to this growth in the global arms trade.[11]

- Technological Advances: states continually upgrade their armed forces in light of the speed of technological advances. This is due to the anarchic nature of the international system whereby states live in real or perceived fear of the ambitions of rivals gaining a military or technological advantage.
- Interstate Conflict: there is no supra-authority in the interstate system to prevent conflict between nations. Therefore, countries continue to prepare for conflict through the purchase of defence systems, hoping that in the roots of this preparation, deterrence, and national protection bloom.
- Maritime Security: the globalisation of trade, dependency on global supply chains and the international nature of modern capital flows have required states to contribute to maritime security, the resilience of sea lanes and sea-lines of communication.
- Economic Growth: emerging powers such as China and the autocratic monarchies of the Middle East are able to satisfy state ambitions for advanced militaries due to the economic growth they have benefitted from in recent decades. There appears to be a link between growth in national exchequers and the rise in a country's military posture.
- Proliferation of the defence market: the activities of defence corporations have multiplied and grown as countries seek to develop their own in-border industrial base in a quest for self-reliance. Defence imports, in this regard, contribute to a nation's capacity for national defence capability generation.
- Symbols of Power: large, defence capital assets like attack aircraft or aircraft carriers are symbols of state power and prestige. Emerging powers seek such artefacts of advanced, first-world statehood and are willing to import such assets to achieve their ambitions.
- Corruption: the large sums involved in defence deals, coupled with a relatively small number of state decision-makers, have marked export deals as especially susceptible to corruption and malpractice. An example is India:[12]

> … the world's top importer of arms over 2008–2017. Various cases of actual or alleged corruption have accompanied some of India's arms contracts over the years. In 2012, the army chief himself alleged that he had been offered a huge bribe over the supply of military vehicles to the army. In 2009, the French press published allegations of corruption over the sale of submarines to Malaysia, which involved the murder of a Mongolian translator who facilitated the deal.

In the case of British defence exports, the practice must be conceptualised in the context of these drivers. For this chapter, the focus falls on corruption as a principal enabler of the arms trade, with this conceptualised, academically, as follows.

Firstly, it is important to remember that the defence sector is not a normal market, subject to open competition and the laws of supply and demand. Rather, it is one of the most regulated global markets in the world, with participants subject to rules relating to competition, value for money, national industrial participation and, at an extreme, security, and treason laws. Countries seek to maintain advanced, autonomous defence design and manufacturing capabilities anchored in local industrial 'hotspots' of production. The reasons for this range from a national desire for strategic freedom of action, the quest for prosperity and economic growth, through to nationalism and prestige. Unfortunately, whatever the motivation, for most countries, the national demand for defence materials and ordnance is far from sufficient to maintain an on-shore sector rich in complex technologies, extensive and exquisite production practices and a continuing demand for capital investment. Defence companies are, therefore, compelled to export to make ends meet, meaning that there could be a large number of businesses from advanced nations seeking a relatively small number of high-value contracts.[13]

In a free market characterised by high-value orders of infrequent number, the dynamics of supply and demand would whittle-down the pursuing pack of companies. Thus, in long-haul civil aerospace, there are only two principal manufactures of large, civilian passenger aircraft: Boeing in the United States and Airbus in Europe. In contrast, there are at least nine manufacturers of major combat air platforms across the globe: Lockheed Martin, Boeing, Northrop Grumman, MiG and Sukhoi in Russia, AVIC in China, and BAE Systems, Airbus, Dassault and Saab in Europe. Little wonder that companies – and governments – might be tempted to go to extremes to win defence export orders.[14] Infrequent orders and vast revenues combine to provide businesses with a perfect storm: a failure to win a major international order could imperil the very survival of the business. In part, as well as advantages of economies of scale and the benefits of pooling and sharing resources, this commercial reality explains why businesses often join together in alliances to develop, market and sell expensive defence equipment.

The World Peace Foundation's Compendium of Arms Trade Corruption contains a number of case studies that unveil many moments of supposed illegality and bad practices during the exports of arms that have been formally investigated since the 1990s. As introduced in Chapter 1, the largest alleged corruption case recorded in the Compendium relates to the Al Yamamah series of arms sales covered by the UK-Saudi Arabia government-to-government deal. The UK's Serious Fraud Office (SFO) uncovered evidence of as much as £6 billion being paid in bribes to officials, the extensive provision of prostitutes and luxury travel offered as inducements to Saudi intermediaries and decision-makers,[15] and the purchase of property and other assets as side-deals to the main programme. The allegations were never tested in a British court as the investigation was cancelled by Prime Minister Blair in 2006: he cited the halt in proceedings as being in the national interest.[16] The academics of the World Peace Foundation concluded that corruption in the arms trade was almost ubiquitous, especially in the case of deals involving major combat aircraft.[17]

Moreover, it can be argued that the UK defence sector's prevalence for the employment of agents in export pursuits can also lead to corrupt practices. Such individuals offer invaluable help in making connections within a buying polity and can provide access to the key, national decision-makers. However, in the United States, for example:[18]

> ... prosecutions in general show that over 90 per cent of corruption cases ... in the history of the FCPA[19] involve agents.

In the arms trade, these women and men (in fact, almost exclusively men) are invaluable because they offer a layer of distance, deniability, and obfuscation if or when law enforcement agencies investigate defence firms.

It is important to note that corruption is not limited to emerging powers in the sense of being clients of defence deals. Rather, European and North American businesses and buyers, historically, have also been implicated. Despite the existence of democratic institutions, supposedly independent judicial systems and a free press, the confidentiality, complexity, and sheer values of defence deals make them susceptible to corruption. But in the developing world, defence exports can yield an important source of political finance:[20]

> ... these deals offer a unique opportunity for steering kickbacks towards ... political operations. Bribes from arms deals are thus often directed towards party political coffers, individual election campaigns, and broader political patronage networks across the political establishment.

Therefore, the manner in which defence export deals can operate has a clear consequence. Where democracies exist, having states enmeshed in corrupt or opaque practices represents a diminution of that democratic intent. Moreover, it entrenches the power and prestige of the, possible, tyrant purchaser seeking greater lethal capacity. The process of concluding defence exports as backroom deals between governments and on-shore commerce can make it impossible for interested parties to make informed judgements on such deals and offers limited scope for proper judicial oversight or media scrutiny:[21]

> All of this makes our hard-won democracies less transparent, accountable and honest. And it results in citizens being unable to determine whether decisions are being made in the national interest, or in some other, narrower interest.

This sense of corruption being an almost ubiquitous feature of arms deals has been well-made over the years by respected institutions such as the World Peace Foundation and campaigners such as CAAT. The historical record of poor practices, clearly speaks for itself. But the UK Bribery Acts of 2010 and 2020 make such practices illegal and contain a specific offense related to bribing a foreign public official. The SFO, since 2010, has been using both Deferred Prosecution Agreements to target wrong-doing and targeted cross-border acts of corruption:[22]

> … the SFO has demonstrated an increasing willingness to use the broad extraterritorial reach of the Bribery Act to pursue cases which span the globe – a trend that will continue.

In addition, UK bribery investigations involve law enforcement agencies from more than one country, and the British have increasingly coordinated actions with anti-corruption enforcers in other legal jurisdictions, especially the US Department of Justice.[23]

In the case of UK businesses themselves, the largest, BAE Systems, following the revelations of the AL Yamamah deals, appointed Lord Woolf[24] and an independent expert review panel in 2007 to explore past ways of working. The remit was to advise on standards of the best ethical business practices, and what the company needed to put in place to achieve them. The Woolf Committee Report was issued in 2008 containing 23 recommendations, which enabled the company to put together a three-year road map for significant improvement.[25]

The result of this is that a case can be made for alleged defence export corruption to be seen in context as part of a particular historical moment which has been addressed, or part-addressed, in recent years. The practices of the late 20th century, some might say, could not work now because of significant internal, institutional reform and the legal powers held through anti-bribery legislation.[26]

That reform has been needed, and seen to be required by businesses, appears to legitimise the academic discourse of unethical practices across the arms trade, at least as a historical phenomenon. It is the lack of openness and (independent from UK Government) oversight of such deals today that allow yesterday's accusations and concerns to recur.

Defence Exports and Ethics: The Case From the Campaign

The Campaign Against the Arms Trade (CAAT), the principal organised lobby group in the UK protesting against defence exports, reject the trade in arms as a matter of principle. The Campaign holds that the resources spent on generating defence systems, components, ordnance, and training solutions for sales to Britain's allies could be diverted into other sectors such as green power, thereby providing a contribution to the UK economy that was based on things other than lethal force.[27]

A key argument from CAAT is centred on the Saudi Arabian-led campaign in Yemen. The civil war there began in 2014 when Houthi insurgents – Shiite rebels with links to Iran – rose up against the Sunni national government. The rebels ousted President Abd Rabbu Mansour Hadi, taking control of the capital city, Sana'a. Since then, interventions by the regional powers – Iran on the side of the rebels and the Saudi-led coalition championing the erstwhile Sunni government – has threatened to draw the country into the wider regional divide between Sunni and Shia communities.[28]

According to the CAAT organisation, since the aerial campaign began in earnest in 2015, about £7.1 billion of arms exports have been made from the United Kingdom to Saudi Arabia. Moreover, since the conflict as a whole was initiated, the total value of sales to Saudi Arabia from the United Kingdom equates to £23.4 billion. For CAAT, the conflict is unethical and the monies earned by the United Kingdom represents a return on trade in death.[29]

There is more to this, however, than just the vast sums involved. CAAT asserts that there are 6,700 BAE Systems employees, suppliers and contractors located in the Middle East that directly support the operations of the Saudi military in their onslaught on Yemen. In addition, under the government-to-government agreement between the UK and Saudi Arabia pertinent to these exports, almost two hundred British military and government civilian officials provide advice, training and support to their Saudi equivalents. Without these personnels and the military equipment and support subject to this agreement, the assertion is that there could have been no effective war in Yemen.

The United Nations estimated in 2022 that two-thirds of Yemen's population, some 20.7 million people required humanitarian assistance, with 12.1 million in 'acute need,' where there was a long-term risk of death through conflict-induced privations. Moreover, in January 2022, some five million people were on the brink of famine, with only immediate aid programmes keeping them alive day-to-day.[30] In terms of the casualties generated by the conflict, in 2022 it was suggested that:[31]

> 131,000 of the estimated 233,000 deaths in Yemen since 2015 are the result of indirect causes like food insecurity and lack of access [to] health

> services ... All sides of the conflict are reported to have violated human rights and international humanitarian law.

The war in Yemen had created the world's worst humanitarian crisis: a global disaster driven, in part, through British defence exports to the Middle East. Whilst there are complex factors involved in this conflict, deliberately not given voice in this work, the scale and regularity of British defence equipment to the Saudi-led coalition pose significant ethical questions to leaders in Whitehall and within British boardrooms.

UK Regional Contribution to Carnage

Having introduced the Saudi Arabian-led coalition's activities in Yemen and, as anti-arms trade campaigners perceive, the human catastrophe as a consequence, the British defence industry contribution to the provision of defence materials is a 'whole of UK' endeavour, embracing all nations and regions. Based on 2020 data, it is assessed that more than 80 companies working from at least 350 UK locations have applied to export equipment to Saudi Arabia, for use in conflicts such as Yemen.[32]

Of those companies, businesses such as Meggitt operate from 44 UK sites. BAE Systems from 141 UK sites, Cobham from 65 UK sites, Chemring from 75 locations, Thales from 28, and Leonardo from 43 sites in the United Kingdom. This, of course, is just a snapshot taken of some well-known commercial names operating in Great Britain and Northern Ireland. But it serves to illustrate that the UK's contribution to carnage in Yemen, from the perspective of CAAT, is institutionalised and embedded right across the country. This should not be a surprise as the commercial defence sector in the UK traditionally accounts for about one percent of gross domestic production and advocates would assert that such a level of activity yields significant social and economic benefits to the nations and regions.[33] This will be explored in subsequent chapters. But the scale of the contribution to conflict, in this case in Yemen, from businesses located in and operating from the UK, appears significant.

Whilst the defence sector in the UK is difficult to access due to commercial-in-confidence agreements and state security rules and protocols, certain data sets have been captured by CAAT and other campaigners. An extract of 50 companies operating from the United Kingdom, who have exported to Saudi Arabia, is summarised at Annex A. Contracts are hard to verify and the numbers generated are drawn from exports' licence data and company reports. The point though, is that such information, even if far from objective in nature, forms part of a strong ethical narrative stitched-through a dominating discourse of UK defence exports, immoral practices and devastating effects.

A hypothesis of this book is that many citizens derive their understandings of UK defence exports and the wider trade in arms and defence materials through the sorts of stories and numbers presented in this chapter. Though selective, subjective and emotive, they are powerful and impactful in society. Other perspectives will be tested in the pages below against this narrative.

Conclusion

The charge sheet against British exports of arms and materials is simple and elegant. First, it is known from recent history that the trade encouraged governmental and commercial illegality and bribery. In so doing, defence exports pervert corporate governance principles and the very organs of the state – both that of the purchaser and supplier. Certain political, commercial and military leaders are revealed to be corrupt, tempted by the arms' dollar, tarnishing colleagues and shattering confidence in the rule of law. Second, the trade is immoral, fuelling and directly enabling conflicts in countries like Yemen. In short, the UK Government and corporate beneficiaries of exports to countries like Saudi Arabia, in the view of the CAAT campaigners, have blood on their hands.

In the following chapters, these charges are set against the other 'truths' that could relate to UK defence exports and deconstructed to sit beside these alternative perspectives. For the moralist, convinced by their cause, other meanings are irrelevant and merely seek to legitimise that which cannot be condoned. Even where this is the case, the following chapters might afford at the very least a window onto the motivations and understandings of those who hold different views on their roles within the practice of British defence exports.

Annex A

Extract of UK Defence and Dual-Use Businesses Support to Saudi Arabia: 50 Businesses

Source Campaign Against the Arms Trade, based on 2020 Data[34]

Ref	*Company*	*Number of UK Company Facilities*
1	Meggitt	44
2	BAE Systems	141
3	Cobham	65
4	Excelitas	41
5	Chemring	75
6	Thales	28
7	Leonardo	43
8	GE	7
9	Honeywell	18
10	Accuracy International	9
11	PW Defence	14

(*Continued*)

Ref	*Company*	*Number of UK Company Facilities*
12	Moog	13
13	Rolls Royce	54
14	Nickwake	1
15	Law Enforcement International	9
16	L3Harris	32
17	Raytheon	62
18	Esterline	28
19	Pyser Optics	21
20	VestGuard UK	4
21	Wesco Aircraft	12
22	Northrop Grumman	16
23	Saywell International	2
24	Curtiss-Wright Controls	8
25	EnerSys	4
26	United Shields International	5
27	UTM	9
28	BCB International	22
29	Martin-Baker	26
30	Herstal Group	5
31	Air and Ground	5
32	AEI Systems	5
33	Wartsila	10
34	Premaberg manufacturing	1
35	Airbus Group	41
36	General Dynamics	28
37	Bioquell UK	14
38	Textron	9
39	ISTEC	8
40	Oxley	16
41	Marshall	18
42	FLIR Systems	26
43	Rangemaster Precision Arms	1
44	Aviation Spares and Repairs	3
45	Hall and Watts Defence Optics	14
46	Rockwell Collins	7
47	Sarkar Defence Solutions	2
48	Cubic	6
49	Gooch and Housego	11
50	South Midlands Communications	6
	Total Number of UK Sites	1,049

Notes

1 Campaign Against the Arms Trade (CAAT), https://caat.org.uk was nominated for the 2021 Nobel Peace Prize. Also, Eric J. Weiner, *The Shadow Market: How Sovereign Wealth Funds Dominate the Global Economy* (Oxford: Oneworld Publications, 2011).

2 Andrew Feinstein, *The Shadow World: Inside the Global Arms Trade* (London: Hamish Hamilton, 2011). The author met with Feinstein in London on 29 July

2013 to discuss his research into alleged corruption associated with defence companies registered in the UK and the role of the UK Government in export sales.

3 *Ibid*, p. xxv.

4 M. Bromley and S, Wezeman, 'transparency in Arms Transfers' in *SIPRI Yearbook 2019* (Oxford: Oxford University Press, 2019).

5 https://www.history.com/this-day-in-history/nelson-mandela-released-from-prison accessed on 4 October 2022.

6 Andrew Feinstein, p. 176.

7 The South African military leadership had a preference for Italian Aermacchi jets for both training and operations.

8 Andrew Feinstein, p. 181.

9 Andrew T.H. Tan, 'Key Drivers of the Arms Trade,' in Andrew T.H. Tan (Ed), *Research Handbook on the Arms Trade* (Cheltenham: Edward Elgar Publishing, 2020) p. 17.

10 The latter at 2014 values. Stockholm International Peace Research Institute (SIPRI), *Military Expenditure Database*.

11 Andrew T.H. Tan. pp: 19–33.

12 Andrew T.H Tan. p. 32.

13 Sam Perlo-Freeman, 'Corruption in the Arms Trade,' in Andrew T.H. Tan (Ed), *Research Handbook on the Arms Trade* (Cheltenham: Edward Elgar Publishing, 2020) pp. 104–6.

14 *Ibid*. p. 105.

15 Andrew Feinstein.

16 David Leppard, 'Blair hit by Saudi "bribery" threat, *Sunday Times*, 19 November 2006.

17 World Peace Foundation, hosted at Tufts University, https://sites.tufts.edu.wpf/

18 Sam Perlo-Freeman, p. 100

19 The US Government's Foreign Corrupt Practices Act.

20 Sam Perlo-Freeman, p. 100

21 Andrew Feinstein, p. 525.

22 Timothy Bowden, Roger A. Burlingame, Matthew L. Mazur and Tom Stroud, *The Anti-Bribery and Corruption Review: United Kingdom – England and Wales* (Dechert LLP, 10 December 2021). https://thelawreviews.co.uk/title/the-anti-bribery-and-abti-corruption-review/united-kingdom-england--wales

23 *Ibid*.

24 Lord Woolf, on appointment, was a former Lord Chief Justice of England and Wales.

25 https://baesystems.com/en-media/uploadFile/20210404031025/1434568989614.pdf

26 BAE Systems has formed an Ethical Leadership Group to continually monitor the Woolf Report implementation, with this work, in turn, overseen and assured independently by advisory groups such as Deloitte.

27 The author spoke with a number of campaigners between August 2021 and August 2022 on condition of anonymity.

28 The Center for Preventive Action, War in Yemen, 4 May 2022, https://www.cfr.org/global-conflict-tracker/conflict/war-yemen accessed 1 September 2022.

29 https://caat.org.uk?homepage/stop-arming-saudi-arabia/uk-arms-to-saudi-arabia/

30 World Food Programme, www.wfp.org https://www.wfp.org/emergencies/yemen-emergency accessed 31 August 2022.

31 Center for Preventive Action, 4 May 2022.

32 Company Data generated by CAAT, https://caat.org.uk/data/companies/.

33 For an assessment of defence industries' contribution, see Henrik Heidenkamp, John Louth and Trevor Taylor, *The Defence Industrial Triptych: Government as Customer, Sponsor and Regulator*, RUSI Whitehall paper 81 (London: Taylor and Francis, 2013).

34 *Ibid*, accessed 5th October 2022. Deliberately, the data has not been verified independently but stands as a campaigner-body assertion of the scale of exports to Saudi Arabia. CAAT did confirm that sites or facilities relate to any working assets of the companies in question from offices and factories through to storage facilities and logistics activities.

3 Geopolitics and Defence Exports

Introduction

The great British foreign secretaries of the early 19th century, Castlereagh, Canning and Palmerston all had one thing in common: they were perceived by contemporary and historian alike as masters of the 'great game' of international relations, especially in their dealings with France, the Austrian Empire, and Tsarist Russia.[1] Yet, for the past two hundred years or so, just what that great game comprised and how it could be captured and conceptualized by an academic discipline has been seen often as confused and dependent upon floating fashions of academic enquiry. Placing the topic of the exports of arms into the currents of discourse that surround international relations needs care.

As the lauded academic Joseph Frankel wrote in the 1980s,[2] books on international relations appear in a variety of guises and constructs. Some writers choose to focus on a scientific explanatory theory of states and politics between them, whilst others prefer to locate their work in what they might describe as 'reality,' something appealing to those academics who value historical enquiry, perhaps. The only unifying understanding is that the subject of international relations is complex, confusing and uncertain.

With this understandable note of caution to guide us, this chapter considers notions of government policy in relation to other states and alliances and critiques the roles played, or otherwise, by actively managed defence exports as a function of geopolitics. We also consider the manner in which overt government policy directs and frames understandings of defence exports, the governmental processes for enabling them, and whether the UK government offers specific benefits or preferences to defence companies, under the banner of effective international relations. In doing so, the chapter provides a framework for accessing the subject of international relations and the place occupied by the sales of weapons systems or their components. The thoughts and lines of enquiry offered through this chapter feed the subsequent chapters of this work and are expanded upon as necessary.

DOI: 10.4324/9781003221494-3

Britain and International Politics

International politics, or the study of the relationships between the states of the world, is a discipline rooted in the political science departments of the world's universities. Significantly, it is also a practice to be found exercised in a country's government buildings as a career option for many well-educated and service-orientated people. In one British government department alone, for example, over a billion pound is spent annually on the management of international relations.[3] By any standard it is an expensive and, possibly, important undertaking. This sense of importance, of course, is the reason so many are attracted to government service in this area of practice in the first place. One would think, therefore, that there would be a consensus around what the subject entailed. We will test that hypothesis shortly.

In the United Kingdom, the main ministries concerned with the topic are the Cabinet Office, the Foreign, Commonwealth and Development Office (FCDO), the MoD and the intelligence agencies. The Prime Minister sets the tone for the foreign policy agenda across the government reflected, perhaps, in the creation of the expanded Office of the Prime Minister with its own Permanent Secretary in 2022. Earlier, during Blair's first days in office between May 1997 and March 1998, the Prime Minister intervened to blunt the Foreign Secretary Robin Cook's supposed 'ethical foreign policy' by vetoing the latter's decision to ban the sale of arms to Indonesia and Saudi Arabia.[4]

Whilst the development and prosecution of foreign policy, as a function of international relations, is a broad governmental responsibility, many analysts would traditionally locate the British Government's expertise in the subject within the FCDO. This department was created on 2 September 2020 as a consequence of the merger of the extant Foreign and Commonwealth Office with the Department for International Development – a management decision described by some development stakeholders as reckless and a dereliction of national leadership.[5] The postulation was that under the combined authority of the new FCDO, less focus would be applied, and less funds made available, to developing nations.

The self-stated role of the FCDO is to:

- Safeguard the UK's national security by countering terrorism, weapons proliferation, and reduce conflict;
- Build national prosperity by increasing exports; and
- Support British nationals around the world through modern and efficient consular services.

Talking informally and on condition of anonymity with some members of the FCDO, little emphasis, or even awareness, was placed on responsibilities for sales.[6] Specifically, defence exports were perceived by some as a direct contradiction of the FCDO's objective of countering weapons proliferation. Indeed, it was suggested that a case could be made that the roles and objectives of the FCDO and DfIT are not wholly inclusive and mutually supportive. This analytical duality, draped in the colours of international relations as an academic discipline and governmental practice, perhaps offers an insight into the topic itself and why it has the ability to frustrate and delight in equal measure.

As this chapter expands, the argument shall be made that the function of exporting military materiel is a lever of international relations and exercised as a deliberate policy imperative. Moreover, as we shall come on to discuss, for a number of theorists, this expansive militarization and endemic economic return is a core objective of the system of international relations itself. The purpose being, supposedly, to benefit certain elites within what is caricatured as the 'military–industrial complex.' For now, suffice to note that it seems strange that the FCDO, the governmental organization responsible for the formulation and exploitation of international political policy, has so little oversight over the management of defence exports within the broader 'game.' It is almost as if the complexities and challenges of designing, manufacturing and selling defence capabilities might fall below, somehow, the lofty thoughts of the practitioners of international relations. Defence exports, though, is a subject that should matter very much to these Whitehall communities as we shall come on to demonstrate.

Accessing and Analysing International Relations

As an academic discipline, the study of International Relations typically seeks to access and, thereby, analyse the international political order through two distinct approaches:

- The state-system method;
- The national-state level of analysis and decision-making.

The first and, possibly most significant, could be characterized as a holistic approach to the topic that encompasses all states and political actors that engage with each other through discernible rules, roles and modes of behaviour. In this sense, system-centric activities and responses become predictable and, therefore, manageable by political leaders and officials. The word 'system' is used deliberately by advocates of this level of analysis as it is comprehensive, embracing all states, stakeholders, values and practices. Moreover, it is an interactive system between peer and partner states, focussing on behaviours and notions of agency. The problem, of course, with such a comprehensive theory of everything is that it is impossible to test and evaluate empirically. That does not stop its advocates, in government buildings and in university departments, from promoting the merits of this theory and its implications for the value made by effective defence exports.

For many analysts, the state-system level of analysis is not an abstract concept, however, in the context of British political decision-making. This country's defence and security policy, from the end of the Second World War onwards, has been a deliberate attempt to maintain a supposed 'balance of power' between the West and, until the 1990s, the Soviet Union. Deterrence theory or the nuclear 'balance of terror' – the doctrine of mutually assured destruction – is an inevitable policy artefact of such thinking. Today, as Russia reasserts itself as a power actor in Europe through its military, following the invasion of Ukraine in 2022, Britain's commitment to exporting defence capabilities to Kiev can be viewed as an attempt to return Europe to a balance of power between nervous Western allies and an aggressive and belligerent Russian state. The same thinking can be applied to the United states' concerns around the economic and military growth of China, and Britain's default policy of alignment to the United States. Hence the supposed 'pivot' of British defence policy to focus on the Indo-Pacific waters and those of the South China Sea – an attempt to contain China through the maintenance of an East-to-West interstate equilibrium: the balance of power:[7]

> The balance of power is therefore an empirical description of how states do act … It is also a recommendation of how states should act.

Under this analysis, Britain's exports of defence equipment and know-how is indeed a mechanism for the maintenance of this interstate balance of power, which lead to reasonable questions around the utility of weapons systems if they exist not for conflict but to prevent conflict as deterrence through strength and preparation. The Campaign for Nuclear Disarmament, for example, would eloquently make the case that nuclear warheads and delivery systems offer a route to the world's destruction via massive nuclear exchanges brought about through miscalculation, arrogance, stupidity, or systems' failures. Such concerns are real and ever-present but seem to champion the notion of a balance of power and maintenance of a rules-based international order as much as critique it. Either way, the flow of technology and defence competencies through, into and from the United Kingdom is an observable feature of the state-system approach to understanding international relations and, as a consequence, cannot be ignored.

The nation-state level of understanding sits below the global-enterprise level of analysis – the state system – with its emphasis on actions within individual countries and decision-making undertaken within borders. In the case of the United Kingdom, this manifests itself, principally, in the statements of defence policy that appear regularly in the public domain. Within a review of geopolitics, this nation-state level of analysis does not focus on the likeness of states and similarity of motives in playing 'the great game' of statecraft, but rather on differences in behaviour and practices: the political system itself, macro-economic considerations, social structures, history, sense of nationalism, religions and education.

For many readers, this sense of a binary choice between analysing geopolitics through a holistic state system lens or through decision-making within borders at the nation-state level may seem like dancing on a pinhead. But it is significant. The state system of analysis promotes an understanding of an objective, and objectified, international environment with rules and practices that can be discerned and mastered. These are codified in part, of course, in elements of international laws, treaties and conventions.[8] At the national level, the real world is the world perceived not modelled – a subjective world – irrespective of the correctness of that perception.[9] British policymaking derives from this subjective understanding of the problems we face: the pseudoscience of an objective, scientific statecraft practiced in government by international relations professionals in fact becomes part of this subjective and contingent understanding of geopolitics. If all knowledge becomes personal and interwoven with identity and self, it could hardly be otherwise.[10]

Better, perhaps, for students of international relations and defence studies to view the international state system as a set of significant environmental factors driving UK defence policies which, of themselves, are subjective and bespoke. After all, the challenges perceived by policymakers are flavoured by both international and local concerns.

For instance, let us take the Dunne Report of 2018.[11] This was an independent study by the former Minister for Defence Procurement, Philip Dunne MP, commissioned by the Secretary of State for Defence, Gavin Williamson. The terms of reference were specific: the Review was to focus on providing an external perspective and challenge to how Defence (the MoD and defence researchers, designers, manufacturers and other contractors) ensures it supports UK economic growth and prosperity. Especially, the work was to capture:[12]

> ... the opportunities for defence exports to make a greater contribution to Defence and the wider UK economy. Realising the opportunities to grow defence inward investment and looking at how defence prosperity can help sustain current and develop new partnerships with industry and our allies.

In many ways, this is a remarkable document. It focuses almost exclusively inwards towards the UK and its regions, looking at economic considerations and national prosperity as objectives in their own right, detached from the doctrines, purposes and roles of the British military. Prosperity, not defence was the principal imperative. As Dunne writes in his foreword:[13]

> As part of the Defence and Security Review 2015, when I was Minister of State for Defence Procurement, the Ministry of Defence was tasked for the first time to include within its formal objectives the promotion of

> prosperity, in line with National Security Objective Three: 'promote our prosperity – seizing opportunities, harnessing innovation to strengthen our national security and working with industry to ensure we have the capabilities and equipment that we need. Our economic and national security go hand-in-hand.

Defence exports are a key ingredient in order to satisfy this ambition.

This focus on inward investment and economic contribution was at a time when the MoD's direct contribution to national GDP was a budget from the public purse of £37 billion per annum as well as support to defence exports of roughly £7 billion generated on average each year – not inconsequential sums of money.[14] The Dunne Report, though, supports those practitioners and academics who view geopolitics as a study of local and national imperatives set into broader international constraints, opportunities and risks. In this regard, national value and contribution to notions of prosperity through defence exports fit well into practices of international relations. In the next section, we consider how such exports are operationalized and managed through governmental oversight and intervention.

Enabling Defence Exports

As introduced in Chapter 1, playing the 'great game' of geopolitics through the lever of defence exports requires a formal exports control policy, a set of government institutions and an overarching process to regulate the practice of exports and approve transactions.[15] In the United Kingdom, this governmental infrastructure of approvals has been described as comprehensive and widespread in both its application and coverage of targeted activities.[16] For example, there are widespread national lists covering military and dual-use technologies, systems and components that require an export licence. Whilst the UK was in the European Union, much of this was coordinated at a European level.[17] Today, whilst the system of controls is national, the content is very much a legacy of the pan-European regime. Roles, though, are very specific and clear: it is the government's responsibility, through the Department for International Trade, to run a process of national regulation that is transparent, efficient and effective. It is the responsibility of the company that wishes to export listed materials or services to ensure that personnel comply with the controls' regime and apply for the relevant export licence. As a chief executive of one small-to-medium-sized business has told the author:[18]

> It is right to have a regulatory framework for the products and technologies I seek to provide to overseas' governments and their militaries. But this regime has to be speedy and efficient. The global economy is dynamic with transactions taken at pace. Control regimes have to be equally dynamic and responsive.

The UK institutions and custodial control of the defence export process was reformed as a consequence of the vote to leave the European Union. Following David Cameron's resignation as prime minister (PM) following the leave vote in 2016, Theresa May was installed as leader of the Conservative Party and new PM. One of the ideas that came from her team – the co-chiefs of staff to the PM, Nick Timothy and Fiona Hill – was the creation of a new government ministry, the Department for International Trade (DIT), principally to negotiate bilateral trade deals with individual countries and international trade blocks.[19] Its first Secretary of State was Liam Fox. It took a while for the Department to establish itself but, under Fox, it developed briefs for trade policy, UK export finance and broader outward investment strategies. It swallowed the UK Trade and Investment organization (UKTI), that part of the erstwhile Foreign Office that was charged with the promotion of exports from the desks of those working within the UK's embassies in overseas' capitals. Significantly, DIT also took control of the Defence Export Services Organization (DESO), so that defence exports were more aligned to the prosperity agenda than, perhaps, of collective defence with and through allies.[20]

DESO morphed into the UK Defence and Security Exports organization (UK DSE) within DIT, emerging with the refreshed mission to champion UK defence and security businesses overseas to achieve export success and market penetration as objectives in their own right. The organization works to build sales opportunities with overseas' governments, promotes UK indigenous defence capabilities and coordinates wider support from across the UK Government to enable national businesses to access overseas' markets. As one UK DSE senior official observed:[21]

> Our work today is more about sales and national prosperity rather than defence collaboration or relationships with allies. That's possibly a change from DESO when it was more about building the defence capabilities of allies and fellow treaty members.

The Director of UK DSE is supported by senior military advisers from the three branches of the armed forces, all experts in the defence capabilities that they seek to promote. Given this, the advisers are more comfortable with established capabilities rather than the innovative and disruptive offerings of emerging defence equipment. As a consequence, those highly technical companies offering something new to the defence market might be at a disadvantage if their contributions are unrecognized by the military specialists within UK DSE.

UK DSE is split into two teams: Region 1 which focuses on the Americas, Pacific and East Asia, and Region 2 which addresses the potential requirements of states in Africa, Europe, the Middle East and Central and South Asia. UK DSE staff within DIT work closely with the MoD and is the lead body in government-to-government commercial arrangements for defence exports. In addition, UK regional trade advisers and defence attaches, working from British embassies, co-ordinate support to UK businesses through UK DSE.

The administrative process through which a UK business seeks an export licence is undertaken almost exclusively online. Firms complete and submit appropriate forms to the DIT to secure a relevant export licence with this being far from a tick-box activity. The civil servants running the process are thorough which businesses can find time-consuming and onerous.[22]

> Larger and even medium-sized firms have to employ specialised staff familiar with the information and process required to deal with [the DIT].

The appropriate desk office in the Department consults with and co-ordinates the actions of other government departments such as the FCDO, MoD, and the security agencies before issuing a decision to the company in question. There is also a significant though separate role played by the MoD in protecting sensitive system information and UK proprietary intellectual property when a firm seeks to export overseas:[23]

> All UK companies must obtain MoD Form 680 approval in order to release information or equipment classified OFFICIAL-SENSITIVE and above to foreign entities.

As can be seen, defence exports are a highly regulated affair with MoD approval for physical and information exchange required along with DIT's approval for the issue of an export licence. Not surprisingly, this rigorous oversight can discourage some business executives from engaging with defence markets, as we shall discuss in subsequent chapters.

So, under the guise of geopolitical international relations, defence exports from the UK reside in a cat's cradle of regulation and oversight despite originating in private sector businesses presumably funded by private capital, borrowings and earnings. The nature of international relations and the lethality of defence systems and materials naturally make this sector subject to bespoke rules. It does not function as a classical free market but, rather, is a sector where the British government acts as sponsor, sometimes customer and always regulator. It is a very particular market indeed with its own culture, rules, processes, and oversights.[24]

The Military–Industrial Complex

Students of international relations will be aware of the concept of the military–industrial complex (MIC): a conspiracy theory that emerged from the United States after the Second World War. It was used by some analysts to explain a variety of events from the disaster of the US involvement in

Vietnam in the 1960s and 1970s through to the size of the US defence budget itself.[25] This thesis holds that munition manufacturers, financiers, the media, think tanks and political elites collude in promoting the conditions and explanations justifying vast public expenditure on defence materials and personnel, with a thriving defence exports market becoming an inevitable consequence.[26]

> This tension meets the needs of the MIC, which has established itself as a very expensive and dangerous kind of Frankenstein, escaping from traditional democratic restraints.

Like all 'theories of everything,' the premise of the MIC is comforting to those who wish to attribute blame to specific groups for the challenges of today. Rather than seeing the world as a complex, imperfect system of multiple drivers and flawed actors, advocates of this thesis believe that the identified components of the MIC deliberately generate international tensions and conflicts.

The military, therefore, have a vested interest in 'peace not breaking out' and the shareholders and senior managers of large, international defence corporations have commercial and personal interests in meeting military demand for technologies, mature systems, spares and upgrades in military capabilities. *Continuing* and bilateral flows between the military and defence industries in personnel, learning, know-how and other exchanges bind the two sides together in a compelling and enduring mutuality. An observable artefact of this, an advocate of the MIC thesis might say, is the number of retired military officers serving in defence industries.

Academics and public intellectuals, and certain figures in the media and print press, also contribute to the MIC by building narratives of defence and security demands, which the military thereafter turn into equipment and support requirements for the industrialist to satisfy. Moreover, the unionized workforce within defence industries advocate policies that promote defence spending through the lens of local and national economic benefits: the more defence exports, the greater the economic returns.

For many observers, such a thesis of MIC collusion is a compelling evocation of vested interest and corruption. As a theory, of course, it is impossible to test or evaluate. Moreover, the 'devil theory' of the MIC is challenged, perhaps, if one is Ukrainian defending the homeland from Russian invasion in the 2020s. the same is true, no doubt, for the Iraqi patriot faced with a Western invasion in 2003.

Conclusions

In this chapter, we have explored complex notions of geopolitics and the international political system and the contributions of British institutions and defence exports to its operation. In accessing and analysing the subject of international relations, we have reviewed notions of a complex, state-level international ecosystem and a more nuanced, view of geopolitics as activities originated within borders and through contingent, imperfect decision-making. In this manner, the practice of defence exports from the United Kingdom is revealed as a set of processes, administrative activities and governmental permissions. Defence exports do not necessarily dance on the international stage, somehow, as performance art demonstrating the historical 'great game' of nations but rather reside in an identified and witnessed bureaucracy, quintessentially British in its undertaking. This, in turn, enables British defence exports to be viewed as a contributory element of relations between the United Kingdom and others.

Some analysts over the years have seen in this governmental–industrial-overseas' customer triptych the kernel of conspiracy, framing a narrative of the so-called military–industrial complex that originated in the United States. Such an overarching and dark theory of everything, anchored in corruption, might be comforting in placing the ills of the world on identified 'bad men' – but it seems glib and fanciful when placed under serious scrutiny. Terrible practices have occurred, as witnessed in the preceding chapter, and will occur again, but these are usually driven and explained by greed, arrogance or other human weaknesses and failings. There is little evidence of systemic conspiracy perpetually housed on the global stage, with defence exports as its operational currency. Rather, as Lord Arbuthnot of Edrom, a previous chair of the House of Commons Defence Select Committee and UK defence minister, argues:[27]

> The relationship between the businesses that contribute to the defence and security of the nation state – that is, the defence industry – and government is critical if citizens are to be kept safe and secure. It is, naturally, a relationship that also often underscores a modern state's foreign-policy stance and sense of place in the world. Yet, despite its clear importance, this subject is seldom properly explored or analysed in a rigorous, clear-eyed manner. Not surprisingly, and perhaps as a consequence, government policies … can seem somewhat contrived, ill-considered and contradictory.

Indeed, this sense of a contradictory and amorphous policy stance might be reinforced as we consider, in the next chapter, defence exports as functions of economic growth and prosperity.

A final thought for this chapter, though, might well be related to utility and purpose. If defence exports from the United Kingdom are seen as a function of geopolitics, then the UK government's approval and licencing of weapons produced in Britain for despatch to Saudi Arabia, for example, must been seen in the light of the UK seeking to influence and support the Saudi authorities. It is in the UK interest, therefore, to have, overtly, Saudi Arabia as an ally, that the UK government through defence sales can mould its behaviours and policies, perhaps nudging it towards supposed Western political and socio-economic norms and standards. Weapons for influence and allegiance, in other words – but does it work for the United Kingdom as a policy imperative?

Russia's attack on the Ukraine in 2022 could be characterized as an enormous geopolitical and security shock to the West. As a consequence, UK policy was developed to support the people of Ukraine and, through the international community, sought to guarantee Ukraine's sovereign integrity. Yet the Saudi Arabian government could be seen to be working actively to undermine sanctions imposed upon Russia and continues to trade with the country. Moreover, Saudi Arabian policies related to oil production seem to align with Russian interests in regard to a restriction in energy provision within the borders of Western powers.[28]

> … in the increasingly hostile energy war between Russia and the West, Saudi Arabia is willing to help Vladimir Putin and snub [the West].

Seemingly, the sale of arms to such states guarantees little in return in the febrile world of international relations other than the stark reality of polities acting in their own perceived national interests – at each decision point leaders arrive at. An observable condition for UK decision-makers to ponder, perhaps, both in regard to bilateral policies with countries such as Saudi Arabia and those relating more broadly to defence exports.

Notes

1 Stephen J. Lee, *Aspects of European History, 1789–1980,* (London: Methuan & Co Ltd, 1982) pp. 37–44.
2 Joseph Frankel, *International Relations in a Changing World* (Oxford: Oxford University Press, 1983).
3 The budget of the FCDO, including capital expenditure was £8.525 billion in 2022–23. https://assets.publishing.service.gov.uk/goverrnment/uploads/system/uploads/attachment_data/file/1075143/FCDO_Main_Estimates_Memorandum_2022-23.pdf
4 See Tom Bower, *Broken Vows: Tony Blair, The Tragedy of Power* (London: Faber and Faber, 2016) p. 64.
5 Tim Shipman, *Fall Out: A Year of Political Mayhem* (London: William Collins, 2017) p. 10.
6 Conversations held throughout 2021.
7 John Spanier, *Games Nations Play: Analysing International Politics* (New York: Holt, Rinehart and Winston, 1984) p. 11.
8 John Fairhurst, *Law of the European Union* (Harlow: Pearson, 2014) pp. 308–314.
9 Spanier, p. 25.
10 Knowledge ref.
11 Philip Dunne MP, *Growing the Contribution of Defence to UK Prosperity, A report for the Secretary of State for Defence* (London: July 2018)
12 *Ibid.,* p. 87.
13 *Ibid* p. 3.

14 *Ibid* p. 5.
15 Jon Lunn, 'The UK legal and Regulatory Framework for UK Arms Exports,' London, House of Commons Library, 4 September 2017, http://researchbriefings.parliament.uk/Research Briefing/Summary/SN02729#fullreport, accessed on 4 October 2017.
16 John Louth and Trevor Taylor, *British Defence in the 21st* Century (Abingdon, Oxon: Routledge, 2019) p. 108.
17 The lists themselves were in law the responsibilities of national governments but coordinated at the European Commission level and subject to agreement under the Wassenaar Arrangement. The latter was formally established in 1996 as a voluntary export control regime whose 42 members exchange information on transfers. The countries are Argentina, Australia, Austria, Belgium, Canada, Croatia, the Czech Republic, Denmark, Estonia, Finland, France, Germany, Greece, Hungary, India, Ireland, Italy, Japan, Latvia, Lithuania, Luxemburg, Malta, Mexico, Netherlands, New Zealand, Norway, Poland, Portugal, Romania, Russia, Slovakia, Slovenia, South Africa, Spain, Sweden, Switzerland, Turkey, Ukraine, the United Kingdom and the United States. It exceeds the borders of the EU, therefore, but the latter is aligned to the agreements recommendations.
18 In discussion with Scott Verney, Chief Executive Officer of Subsea Craft Ltd, on 22 June 2022.
19 Tim Shipman, *Fall Out: A Year of Political Mayhem,* p. 10.
20 See MoD, *British Defence Doctrine: Joint Warfare Publication (JWP 0–01)* (London: MoD, 1996).
21 A senior UK DSE official speaking with the author on 15th February 2022, on the condition of anonymity.
22 Louth and Taylor, p. 109.
23 Ministry of Defence, 'Ministry of Defence (MOD) Form 680 applications,' www.gov.uk/guidance/mod-f680-applications, accessed 1 January 2018 and again 7 July 2022.
24 Henrik Heidenkamp, John Louth and Trevor Taylor, *The Defence Industrial Triptych: Government as Customer, Sponsor and Regulator* (London: RUSI Whitehall paper 81, 2013).
25 K. J. Holsti, *International Politics: A Framework for Analysis* (Englewood Cliffs, NJ: Prentice-Hall, 1983) pp. 6–15.
26 Spanier, p. 401.
27 Heidenkamp et. al. *Foreword* p. 1.
28 Jack Farchy, Annmarie Hordern and Ben Bartenstein, *Saudi Arabia Snubs Biden and Aids Putin with Oil Output Cut* (London: Bloomberg UK, 5 October 2022). https://www.bloomberg.com.news/articles/2022-10-05/saudi-arabia-enrages-biden-and-aids-putin-with-oil-output-cut

4 National Economic Prosperity and Defence Exports

Introduction

The Strategic Defence and Security Review 2015 (SDSR 15)[1] introduced the notion of national prosperity as a defence objective. This meant, presumably, that the health and wellbeing of defence businesses located in the United Kingdom, their sales to the MoD and exports to friendly nationals, became a national mission. Moreover, the Defence and Security Industrial Strategy (DSIS) of 2021[2] reemphasized the significance of the prosperity agenda and signalled that a new 'industrial participation' or 'offset strategy' was under consideration. This would contribute to the formulation of a post-Brexit national security framework, centred on exports, to build a sustainable and affordable set of military capabilities for use in the United Kingdom, enabled by sales overseas, thereby contributing to the parallel objectives for the MoD of national safety and physical security and, critically, economic prosperity.

This chapter considers the case for prosperity in the context of UK defence exports. It considers the case being made for prosperity and the contributions defence businesses could or should make. The work goes on to consider the arguments made in an independent report to the Defence Secretary by Philip Dunne MP in 2018 and, further, analyses a refreshed interest by the British Government in defence 'offsets.' It considers and questions the impact of an inward industrial participation policy on outward export campaigns. Lastly, it addresses the difference in emphasis between notions of prosperity at a national level and defence prosperity as a local phenomenon.

Trade, exports and benefits received and distributed nationally – prosperity, if you will, are features of the international system that are as old as the hills.[3] Defence exports have been used often to achieve high policy goals of national security whilst, concurrently, maximizing returns received on the utilization of public finances and private capital. How such notions have been reconfigured for use in the 21st century is the crux of the enquiry in this chapter.

DOI: 10.4324/9781003221494-4

The Case for Prosperity

Defence exports are generated typically by the actions of businesses, who have a say in what they produce and the practices through which they operate. This may not always seem apparent to governments around the world.[4] Rather, political leaders might be tempted to treat defence firms, and their exports, as organs of geopolitical policy, as we discussed in the preceding chapter.

An economist might have a simple approach to businesses, commencing with the consideration of the following: firms are concerned with the transformation of inputs to outputs through a variety of processes. Inputs cost a firm money (indeed, cash is an input in its own right) and outputs earn money. The margin between earned revenues and the costs incurred against specific outputs or products constitutes the profit of a firm. To maximize this profit, which the providers of capital (shareholders and lenders) require, senior managers in a business are faced with a multitude of choices and decisions to make:[5]

> ... choices of what types of output to produce, how much to produce and at what price; choices of what techniques of production to use, how many workers to employ and of what type, what suppliers to use for raw materials, equipment etc. In each case, when weighing up alternatives, managers will want to make the best choices.

For our typical business economist, studying and reviewing what are, essentially, the choices made by businesses, notions of broad national prosperity seldom, if ever, feature. Rather, the study focus will be usually on influencers such as the macro-economic environment, the internal health and condition of the firm, and the external effects of business decision-making. The economic researcher might conclude that capitalism and free markets are not concerned, principally, with the economic common good of all in a nation, equally distributed. It might seem odd in many ways, therefore, to equate UK defence activities, and exports in particular, to notions of national prosperity: shareholder returns, yes, but to increases in economic and social benefits to all?

To make sense of this, it is important to note that UK defence industries reside in a highly regulated market that possesses specific controls and burdens on firms. For a company, the generation of inputs to defence material outputs is not left to the hidden hand of markets alone, as Adam Smith would have it.[6] Instead, for businesses that operate within the defence sector, the hidden hand is sheathed in a glove of governmental stewardship – with the Government acting as customer, sponsor and regulator of the sector.[7] This allows, in turn, the British Government to generate policy that a contribution to national prosperity, principally through exports, is a requirement of the defence sector in the United Kingdom, and the individual businesses that operate within it.

Reframing Government for Defence

Most people would probably regard the British Government, and its armed forces, as the main customer of businesses operating in the defence sector of this country. The British Government is conceptualized in an uncomplicated manner as 'customer.' It is easy to perceive how, from a company's point of view, exports of the same goods to overseas' nations are obviously sensible. The business is acting merely in its own commercial interest by expanding its client base. So, governments as customers is an obvious and highly relevant concept to the commerce–state relationship.

Whilst easily understandable, it is not, though, the only feature of the government-industry relationship. Governments frequently sponsor the activities of onshore defence companies, offering a set of advantages to businesses not seen in parallel commercial sectors. One such advantage can be found in the field of research and development. Market imperfections and multiple commercial priorities for the use of capital are conditions unlikely to generate all of the general and applied research needed for a country's future defence posture and military capabilities. Rather, historically, government has pump-primed commercial research through direct funding and grants. Indeed, as part of DSIS 21, £6.6 billion was set to be spent on research and development with the private sector over ten years.[8]

Collaborative and international defence research programmes, especially, are mediated and choreographed by governments.[9] This broad 'stewardship' by the British Government of onshore defence businesses expands to cover preferences in procurement choices and trade and commercial assistance through British embassies and high commissions. In such a manner, the British Government is able to act as both customer and sponsor.

In addition to these two roles, it is important to note that the defence sector is highly regulated and the domestic government has the part to play here as well. The sector is subject to national and international treaty obligations and regulations, as well as a raft of rules, conventions and norms which businesses must follow. Commercial freedom of action is framed and constrained by this governmental architecture of control. In 2012, for example, BAE Systems and EADS (Airbus) wished to merge, a move that was greeted with some excitement in the market. In contrast, the future Defence Secretary, Ben Wallace, as an MP in 2012, argued that it was not a decision for markets but for politicians.[10] Indeed, his view prevailed, as:[11]

> BAE and EADS were forced to abandon £30 billion merger talks earlier this month after the German Chancellor Angela Merkel personally intervened to block a deal.

As well as acting as a customer and sponsor, the British Government (along with other governments) embraces this regulatory role and intervenes to shape the strategies of British defence businesses. Put simply, this is because:[12]

> Defence industries are still regarded as part of a country's arsenal: a repository of goods, services, know-how and manpower from which a military can draw in conflict ... Industry is not just democracy's arsenal – it is democracy's operational partner meaning that much of today's military competencies actually reside in the industrial base.

It can be seen that the relationship between the Government and its onshore defence businesses is complex and multi-faceted. The quest for contribution towards national prosperity must be seen in this context, with the value-added being the economic benefits being received through defence exports.

Prosperity: The Defence Contribution

As introduced in earlier chapters, in 2018 the MoD tried to take a stand on growing the contribution of the defence sector to UK prosperity. A previous minister for defence procurement, Philip Dunne MP, was tasked with producing a report that would set out a policy framework for growth.[13] It was in many ways a direct response to the defence task relating to prosperity articulated in SDSR 15. The Dunne Report was an attempt by the British Government to go beyond the MoD to articulate the contribution made by the constituent parts of defence – MoD, the armed forces and, critically, industry – to UK economic growth and prosperity. It made the case that the contribution of defence was considerable, when perceived as a public–private enterprise,[14] rooted as it was at the time in a defence budget of £37 billion and identified defence exports in excess of £7 billion. The argument made by the report was powerful, noting three distinct areas of analysis around which 41 recommendations were made:[15]

- The contribution of the defence enterprise to national prosperity and growth is generally unrecognized and taken for granted by society. The input from defence exports is considerable and has the potential to grow the UK's prosperity further still. To do this, however, the Government needs to embed the concept of decision-making for prosperity across all of its defence activities, especially those associated with acquisition of capabilities. In this regard, MoD needs to actively prioritize and promote exports.
- Defence as an enterprise needs to be more agile and less process driven. The sense was that a burden of bureaucracy, excess processes and lengthy staffing of options was holding defence back thereby limiting the contribution it could make to national prosperity.
- The relationship between defence industries and the rest of the economy and society is misunderstood and needs to be conceptualized for decision-makers and those providing private capital or public funds. For example, there is a strong historical correlation between research,

applied research and development, located in defence, and technological innovation and advancement in civil society.

This last point, in particular, is especially important. In the United States and across many of its Western allies, since the end of the Second World War, the national security strategy was based on being technologically superior to known or potential enemies. The West, led by the United States:[16]

> … decided to offset the Soviet Union's quantitative military superiority not by building bigger armies but … by investing in technology.

Decision makers in the United Kingdom sought to stay close to the United States and support its role as the hegemonic lead in the post-Cold War world order, in many ways, to secure access to that country's technologies.[17] The Dunne Report's emphasis on onshore UK technological development was significant in this regard, recognizing that national prosperity does not thrive necessarily with a security stance based on technological dependency on another state.

The 41 Recommendations from the Dunne Report, summarized at Annex A, are sensible and offer a service of good husbandry to the MoD and its industrial partners and suppliers. Yet a quick review suggests that they hardly represent a dynamic new strategy for growth and economic prosperity – championed by the defence enterprise through overseas' sales. Indeed, tracking the progress of these recommendations was not promoted by the DSIS and, consequently, not prioritized by the MoD.[18] It was as if Dunne had drafted a worthy though unspectacular recipe of solid ingredients which the MoD chefs couldn't be bothered to make.

National Prosperity Contribution and Local Imperatives

As highlighted by Dunne's work, the UK Government is limited in its approach to promote and manage defence activities, especially exports, for domestic prosperity, by its lack of data. Within any organization or complex system, information gathering, processing, sifting and presenting pertains to control: the lifeblood of systems' theory and organizational design.[19] Put glibly, if something is not being measured it is most certainly not being managed. This management information is critical in government if a policy is to be actively worked, targets met and effects credibly assured: a weakness still haunting the MoD.

Data and management information do exist in the private sector and points to the impact of defence on society. BAE Systems, for example, regularly commissions the research company Oxford Economics to report on the company's economic and social contribution to the United Kingdom. This is especially important for company executives. Since 2021, UK Government procurement competitions are required to allocate at least ten percent of the marks available for assessment to the following themes of social value:

- The contribution to recovery from the Covid-19 pandemic and associated economic shock;
- Addressing economic inequalities;
- Tackling climate change;
- The promotion of equal opportunities between the nations and regions; and
- Enhancing wellbeing and social integration across communities.

A brief analysis of these five points of 'social value' suggests that the focus rests especially at the local level.

The 2022 Report from Oxford Economics[20] focuses on social value, as defined above, but also promotes BAE Systems' investments in recruitment, training and personnel development. Defence programmes and projects are often multi-year, even multi-generational, affairs, and rest on the abilities and skills of employees to execute effectively. Recruitment, retention, and refreshment policies and practices are critical if defence businesses are to be successful:[21]

> In 2022, the company plans to recruit 900 apprentices and 450 graduates. For young people, these are major opportunities to earn and secure a well-paid living over a sustained period. BAE Systems is not alone in its commitment to apprenticeships, as visits to websites of Rolls Royce, MBDA, Babcock and other defence suppliers underline.

The line of logic linking defence to prosperity seems to run as follows. Defence equipment manufacturing and support activities in the United Kingdom are well funded by the British Government in terms of providing capabilities for its own armed forces. This is amplified significantly by overseas' sales. Indeed, revenues from sales to the UK military alone would not be enough to cover the investments necessary in research and development, facilities and employee costs to keep many defence companies thriving. Combined income from UK sales and exports land locally, financing well-paid jobs across the region. For the company, this contributes to the confidence necessary for expansion, more recruitment and further training. As those employees within the region in question typically live and consume locally, prosperity is maintained or rises (or economic decline is resisted). This is critical, as we shall see shortly, where the defence prime contractor, and its immediate supply chain, are the main employers in a town or area.

Sticking with BAE Systems for the moment, the company, its suppliers and respective workforces paid close to £1.6 billion in direct taxation in 2020. Beyond this, through consumer spending, the workers involved contributed an additional £1.0 billion to the UK Exchequer over this period.

The company received £3.8 billion in payments from the UK government for the tax year ending in 2020: the contribution to national and local prosperity from such an investment, plus the monies returned to the British Government through taxation, is hugely important.[22] Over the same period, though, BAE Systems alone had exports of £4.5 billion – almost a fifth more than UK revenues.[23] The link between exports and prosperity seems obvious and significant. As Mike Formosa, the Managing Partner of Renaissance Strategic Partners, a global defence strategy advisory firm, states:[24]

> It is important that defence is viewed as economic activity as well as activities focussed on generating defence capabilities. These two themes need to be in harmony if defence programmes are to succeed. The returns from exports or international collaborations are hugely important in this context.

Prosperity and lethality, perhaps, are two sides of the same coin.

Barrow and BAE Systems: A Local Example

These themes can be encapsulated through a quick review of the operations in Barrow-in-Furness in Cumbria. Sir Roger Carr, the chairman of BAE Systems, notes in his foreword to the 2022 economic impact report from Oxford Economics that, in building nuclear-powered submarines in Barrow-in-Furness:[25]

> … we employ 26 percent of the working population. In 2020, we spent nearly £700 million with suppliers in the nation's most deprived local authorities … I am very proud to be Chairman of a company which makes such a significant contribution to the collective security and prosperity of our nation.

Sir Roger's pride sits on some fascination corporate targets, statistics, and assertions:[26]

- The company has a programme to develop, with the MoD, sustainable technologies for use across the defence footprint;
- It has a target of achieving net zero greenhouse gas emissions from all of its operations by 2030;
- Average productivity per worker is calculated at £83,000, 29 percent higher than the overall average per worker from across the UK economy.
- 190 senior leaders drawn from BAE Systems' business groups mentor 200 different SMEs, leading to an estimated productivity boost to the economy of £12.2 million.

It seems that the contribution made by defence exports to notions of national prosperity is predicated on defence businesses being successful locally, as customers, employers, tax payers and sponsors of good practices. In Barrow-in-Furness, and throughout Cumbria as a whole, BAE Systems spends over £80 million per annum via a 100, or more, local suppliers. A quarter of all manufacturing jobs in the county exist because of BAE Systems' operations.[27] Moreover, Barrow, itself, is a company town: its wellbeing, future prosperity and, indeed, identity is interwoven with that of BAE Systems.[28]

> The sheer immensity of the shipyard, which traverses the entire length of Barrow Island, obscuring the view of the Irish Sea for the residents of Barrow, is visible from almost everywhere in town – a physical reality, symbolic of its identity. Every main street appears to lead to the shipyard; all businesses cater to it or provide services for its workers; and every statue or plaque remembers a great man or event invariably connected with the work down at the dock.

The capillary and amorphous nature of 'prosperity' flows from local, through national to international domains and returns again, with the regularity of tides. That these flows find a channel through defence exports is no surprise: ideas of security and prosperity are trans-border concepts, after all.[29]

In this regard, it is interesting that BAE Systems was one of a number of possible villains unveiled through a harsh, though, compelling narrative in Chapter 2. This current chapter, in contrast, suggests that a more nuanced judgement can be made on such companies that exist, in part, through defence exports and international collaborations. For folk in Barrow, for example, BAE Systems helps to shape, for the better, their identity, life chances and happiness: the opposite, perhaps, of what a villain would aspire to do.

Offsets and Industrial Participation

The subject of defence offsets is an interesting concept. At its most basic, the topic can be defined as a sort of reciprocal investment: when a country purchases defence materials from within another country's jurisdiction, the acquiring government requires an additional 'offsetting' investment into it from the vendor to compensate the country for the high costs of defence acquisition.[30]

> Contemporary arms sales, therefore, invariably comprise two parallel transactions: the first is the primary defence contract involving the procurement of military systems, based on conventional price-quality considerations, and the second is the offset deal, whereby suppliers compete on the worth of their respective investment packages.

The offset proposal may well relate to the defence contract itself, committing the company, perhaps, to onshore production of the weapons procured through an investment into a new factory, training and increased employment opportunities within a local area. US-registered firm General Dynamics, for instance, sale of the Ajax suite of armoured vehicles to the United Kingdom was predicated on factory production and trials in South Wales, an area of post-industrial depravation. Or, the offset in question could have a non-defence component, such as investment in technical education, blue-sky research or infrastructure development.

The UK's first formal inward offset policy was a child of the 1990s, masquerading as a policy of 'industrial participation.' This approach was abandoned in 2012 following the European Procurement Directive which quashed the concepts of offsets in Europe. However, this fusion of defence, development and prosperity has resurfaced with the DSIS of 2021, confirming that, post-Brexit, a refreshed offset policy is under consideration.[31]

The text comes on to explore offsets and industrial participation more fully in the chapter relating to technology transfer and international development. But, it is important to note here that national prosperity and regional development, through defence activities in the United Kingdom, might not be just related to exports. An emerging policy of inwards' directed offsets and industrial participation through defence imports – international defence firms coming to the United Kingdom – might have a role to play as well.

Conclusions

In this chapter, we have explored ideas around national prosperity through defence exports. The chapter started with notions of commercial interests driving defence activities before introducing ideas relating to British Government oversight and governance of the defence sector. In this regard, the activities of government were revealed as sponsoring and directing defence businesses, with the latter residing in a complex web of permissions and regulations. This had been reframed by the government to make prosperity a defence mission and responsibility, in part, of the defence industrialist. In many ways, this was expressed overtly through the Dunne Report of 2018: paradoxically, the conclusions from that work do not appear to have flowed through seamlessly into the findings of the DSIS in 2021.

Local perspectives relating to prosperity and regional development were explored through a review of the economic and social activities at Barrow-in-Furness, and the role played by BAE Systems at the heart of the town. Finally, a word of caution was introduced relating to the importance and impact of offsets and broader industrial participation. In short, in the future, imports rather than exports might contribute more overtly to prosperity through the application of a refreshed offset policy, flagged in the DSIS.

Here, too, there are challenges. For the British Government, purchasing defence capabilities to enable a set of offset benefits, the procurement would be undertaken typically by the UK procurement agency, currently the Defence Equipment and Support organization (DE&S). The role of UK defence acquisition is considered in the chapter on military co-operation but, it would be fair to state, not all stakeholders admire its performance. As Mark Francois, chairman of the Conservative Party's European Research Group, ex-defence minister, and member of the House of Commons Defence Select Committee would have it:[32]

> We just don't seem to learn from our mistakes with defence acquisition. That might undermine grand plans for security through exports and [inward] collaboration outlined by the IR and DSIS.

In seems clear, however, that, at some level, defence exports do contribute to notions of national and local prosperity and economic contribution. The book considers next the proposition that such an outcome is the consequence of normal commercial supply and demand imperatives and the pursuit of a defence company's self-interest.

Annex A

The Dunne Report 2018: Summary of Recommendations

The recommendations from the Dunne Report are summarized below. For a comprehensive treatment of each point, please refer to the Report itself, pp. 56–59.

Number	*Recommendation*
1	The Office of National Statistics should gather more information about spending on defence across the economy.
2	Independent research should be commissioned by the MoD to identify the total economic benefit.
3	The MoD should help strengthen the Defence Sales Organization.
4	Industry needs to show more leadership in driving a single Team UK approach.
5	Incentives should be developed for the armed forces to provide strategic support for defence exports.
6	Greater engagement between MoD and the Treasury to provide training and other enablers for defence exports.
7	Proposals should be developed to enable the industry to access UK test and evaluation facilities to support exports.
8	The defence enterprise should manage risks more effectively and take a more strategic view of mitigations.
9	Metrics and other forms of measurement need to be developed to effectively consider prosperity proposals.

(*Continued*)

Number	*Recommendation*
10	MoD should focus on technical education, skills and training.
11	A common approach to data collection needs to be developed.
12	MoD should resource its responsibilities for managing prosperity more effectively.
13	MoD should increase and champion procurement agility.
14	MoD should publish how much it invests in its workforce.
15	MoD and industry need to improve their evidence base relating to future skills.
16	Independent research needs to be undertaken on the social and financial impacts of defence expenditure.
17	Employment flexibility should be considered for skills retention.
18	The MoD should improve the data it collects on Service leavers relating to skills, qualifications and salaries.
19	MoD to consider whether its spend on science and technology is sufficient.
20	Innovation Fund spending needs to be prioritized and its profile enhanced.
21	MoD should retain its priority for driving innovation.
22	MoD should adopt an open architecture across the defence spectrum.
23	Innovation needs to become a larger element of bigger procurement programmes and projects.
24	Defence needs to incorporate a greater appetite for risk in innovation.
25	MoD needs to find a more equitable way to share risks and rewards with the industry.
26	MoD should expand its work to encourage more businesses into the defence sector.
27	Intellectual property issues need to be solved.
28	MoD needs to share intelligence and intentions with the industry at an early stage.
29	Emerging procurement practices should be blended with existing organizations to speed up acquisitions of capabilities.
30	Defence needs to access MilTech investors and development capital.
31	MoD needs to harness regional expertise and strengths.
32	MoD needs to consult more with BEIS and local communities when considering local projects.
33	MoD needs to enhance its international engagement approaches and adopt the same approach for home acquisitions.
34	When developing selection criteria for new procurements, the prosperity impact across the UK needs to feature.
35	MoD needs to ensure it has freedom or manoeuvre, post-Brexit.
36	Major procurements, post-Brexit need to be considered.
37	The MoD should commission independent research on tax revenues and prosperity.
38	MoD and industry to consider how relationships could work better.
39	MoD's financial framework should yield more flexibility to encourage training institutions to be more entrepreneurial.
40	MoD and the Treasury should work together to reduce burdensome VAT administration.
41	MoD needs to publish regularly details of its regional footprint and prosperity impact.

Notes

1 HM Government, *National Security Strategy and Strategic Defence and Security Review 2015*, Cm 9161 (London: The Stationery Office, 2015).
2 Ministry of Defence (MoD), *Defence and Security Industrial Strategy: A Strategic Approach to the UK's Defence and Security Industrial Sectors*, CP 410 (London: The Stationery Office, 2021).
3 John Spanier, *Games Nations Play* (New York N.Y: Holt, Rinehart and Winston, 1984) pp. 77–79.
4 Per Lundin, Niklas Stenlas and Johan Gribbe (Eds), *Science for Welfare and Warfare: Technology and State Initiative in Cold War Sweden* (Sagamore Beach MA: Science History Publications, 2010).
5 John Sloman, Kevin Hinde and Dean Garratt, *Economics for Business* (London: Pearson, 2013) p. 5.
6 Adam Smith, *An Inquiry into the Nature and Causes of the Wealth of Nations* (Sheba Blake Publishing e-book, 2018).
7 Henrik Heidenkamp, John Louth and Trevor Taylor, *The Defence Industrial Triptych: Government as Customer, Sponsor and Regulator, (RUSI Whitehall Paper 81),* (Abingdon OXON: Routledge, 2013).
8 Ministry of Defence (MoD), *Defence and Security Industrial Strategy: A Strategic Approach to the UK's Defence and Security Industrial Sectors*, CP 410 (London: The Stationery Office, 2021).
9 Alastair Cameron (Ed), "Defence Research and Development in the Atlantic Nations," *RUSI Occasional Paper, 2*007.
10 The author debated the merits of the proposed transactions with Ben Wallace MP, the future Secretary of State for Defence, on occasions on the Today Programme, BBC Radio 4 in 2012.
11 Angela Monaghan, 'BAE-EADS Merger a Missed Opportunity,' *Daily Telegraph*, 23 October 2012.
12 Heidenkamp et al., p. 3.
13 Philip Dunne MP, *Growing the Contribution of Defence to UK Prosperity: A Report for the Secretary of State for Defence* (London: MoD, July 2018).
14 John Louth and Trevor Taylor, *Beyond the Whole Force: The Concept of the Defence Extended Enterprise and Its Implications for the Ministry of Defence* (London: RUSI, 2015).
15 The 41 recommendations from the Dunne Report are summarized at Annex A to this chapter.
16 Jacques S. Gansler, *Democracy's Arsenal: Creating a Twenty-First Century Defense Industry* (Cambridge, MA: The MIT Press, 2011) p. 253.
17 Michael Clarke, *The Challenge of Defending Britain* (Manchester: Manchester University Press, 2019) p. 74.
18 The Dunne Report recommendations were not taken forward by the DSIS and a senior civil servant, speaking to the author on 28 March 2022 on condition of anonymity, confirmed that progress was not being tracked.
19 Richard L. Daft, *Organization Theory and Design* (New York, NY: West Publishing Company, 1995) p. 311
20 Oxford Economics, *BAE Systems' Contribution to the UK Economy: An Independent Report by Oxford Economics, 2022* (London: BAE Systems, 2022)
21 Trevor Taylor, 'A New Report Reveals the Significant Contribution of BAE Systems to the UK's Economy and Society,' *RUSI Commentary – the 5 Minute Read* (London: RUSI, 31 January 2022).
22 Oxford Economics, pp. 55–59.
23 Ibid., pp. 65–68.
24 Mike Formosa, in conversation with the author in London, 19 July 2022.

25 Oxford Economics, p. 2.
26 Ibid, based on 2020 figures.
27 Ibid, p. 74.
28 Lauren Twort and Gabriela Thompson, 'The Twenty-First Century Armoury: A Town called Barrow,' in *The RUSI Journal* (London: Routledge, 2017) p. 4.
29 Patrick Porter, *The Global Village Myth: Distance, War and the Limits of Power* (London: Hurst and Company, 2015).
30 Ron Matthews and Jonata Anicetti, 'Offset in a Post-Brexit World,' in *The RUSI Journal*, 2021, No. 5, p. 50.
31 MoD DSIS, p. 51.
32 Rt. Hon. Mark Francois MP, interviewed on 26th July 2022, in London.

5 Defence Exports: A Function of Business and Commerce

Introduction

As we have seen in earlier chapters, many citizens respond to ideas associated with defence exports through an emotive language framed in the arms' trade as being associated with 'merchants of death.' The merchants themselves, operating in the large and small commercial organizations that form the defence enterprise in the United Kingdom, not surprisingly view their work in a different context. Following on from the brief visit to Barrow-in-Furness a few pages ago, the folk from there might suggest that:[1]

> The inextricability of the yard from the identity of the people of Barrow, and vice versa, has resulted in a proud, tight-knit and protective community. One Barrovian encapsulated it all: proud of their hard graft – 'that's what a lot of Barrow did – manual work – and that's something to be proud of.'

Put simply, the workers employed by such companies find themselves on the shop floor in manual roles or in professions that service the company, the defence sector and their local communities. They are proud of their work. Notions of 'unethical practices' or 'trades in death' are not a taxonomy to be found in the mouths of workers in these businesses. Also, the professions being practiced across a BAE Systems' factory in Barrow may also feature in the non-defence sector as well: accountancy is accountancy wherever it is undertaken. For some professional people within companies such as BAE Systems, QinetiQ or Babcock, it is the execution of the profession rather than the purpose of the business that is the allure. For others, there is a sense of loyalty to the company, the British military that they serve and the region within which they live and work. Despite those promoting a 'merchants of death' narrative, sales to far-away lands may not be at the forefront of consciousness when working in the UK defence sector.

In contrast, perhaps, for board members and senior executives, motivations might be multiple, nuanced and complex, tied-up with their own potential for remuneration, professional growth, and reputations. One such

DOI: 10.4324/9781003221494-5

motivation for a chief executive is to serve the interests of shareholders through sales, maximizing profits, growth in market share and new market penetration. Exports, as a consequence of this, may well feature highly on the agenda of a typical C-suite[2] in the defence sector.

For the people at the top of a company, the focus is principally on activities that grow turnover, yield profits, offer appropriate returns to investors and generate an effective pipeline for future orders and development opportunities. It would be commercial incompetence not to target, or even prioritize, overseas' business development and sales in this regard. At one level, the company may view itself as a private sector component of Britain's armoury helping to keep the country secure but, first and foremost, it is a business subject to normal commercial dynamics. The existence of, and quest for, defence exports must be regarded through this lens.

If this is reasonable, defence exports should be purged of the veneer of geopolitics and ideas associated with British prosperity. Whilst the activities of defence businesses are monitored by the state through an appropriate framework of permissions, the drivers for the exports of lethal capabilities are financial not geopolitical. Moreover, in this analysis, the choreography and mission intent of such exports is directed from the boardroom not the ministry. Ministers and government officials seemingly misunderstand this – whether through blinkered or opaque eyes it is hard to understand.

This chapter considers and critiques the proposition that defence exports from the United Kingdom represent merely the function of sound business management: a deliberate ambition to sell as much product as possible at the most beneficial price, irrespective of the wider possible impacts of such trades. It goes on to locate this commercial imperative within ideas of professional commercial practice and complex interdependencies across the defence enterprise itself. It then considers a more nuanced relationship between the government, military clients and the business community. Through this, the significance of commercial research and development to this business relationship with the government, and therefore sales beyond Britain's borders, is introduced. The chapter begins, however, with a consideration of just what a business is, how it should be conceptualized for defence and what its purposes should be. Obvious ones, perhaps, but questions that seem seldom asked in defence circles or taught on courses on defence strategy or international relations.

The Business of Defence

The Nature of a Business Organization

Richard L. Daft was an internationally renowned academic working out of Vanderbilt University at the turn of the century. His principal areas of research were organizational theory and design and the role of the business in society. Daft's basic premise was that a business is hard to academically access and understand as a complete, single entity, but rather:[3]

> ... we see outcroppings, such as a tall building or a computer workstation or a friendly employee.

This idea of an organization as a whole, however, was perceived to be vague and abstract. The business could be typically scattered around several locations and across multiple legal domains. Given this, for researchers to understand a business organization, or for governments to attempt to regulate such entities, policymakers and analysts have to note the four central characteristics that are common to all:[4]

- Businesses are social entities composed of individuals and groups of people. The building blocks of businesses are these people and the roles they perform within and across specific specialisms. The skills and competencies of these people inform the culture of the organization along with its history, values and the stories being told of the business.
- The business is goal directed and established for a purpose. Whilst there are typically multiple stakeholders and interests, the guiding purpose is usually financial, expressed as short- and long-term financial goals.
- The business is a deliberately constructed set of activities for groups or individuals to perform. The structure of the organization, its organizational chart and relationships between professional groupings, all contribute to its identity and sense of purpose of its employees.
- Historically, businesses were identified by boundaries that separated them from other organizations: membership was distinct, targeted and framed by contracts of employment, team and personal objectives, performance indicators, and other such artefacts. Today, the boundaries of competitive companies, their supply chains and customers, are becoming permeable and amorphous. Information, components, technologies and even employees are shared as businesses increasingly collaborate to generate commercial effects greater than those being projected by individual commercial contributions alone.

This is significant as the study of a business was traditionally undertaken through notions of organisations as 'closed systems.' These are systems which are autonomous, enclosed and not interacting with external organizations or influences. Early management concepts flowing from the industrial revolution, including scientific management, adopted closed-systems' approaches as they assumed that the business could be made more effective and efficient solely through internal design and inward-looking management.

Today, scholars view businesses as open systems interacting with, shaping and being shaped by, broader forces in the economy and society at large. Conceptually and as a matter of common sense, a business cannot seal itself off from its socio-economic environment but must adapt and continually change if it is to survive.[5] A defence business in the United Kingdom, consequently, is a shift-shaping member of a broad defence ecosystem comprised of many peoples, brands, borders and influences. If this is reasonable, to frame simply a defence business through its exports 'as merchants of death' is to take but one route through an ever-changing landscape that has many paths.

The Profit Motive

It seems obvious to suggest that a piece of defence equipment such as a tank, for example, cannot be produced by one person in isolation. Irrespective of whether the intended users of the tank are British Army personnel or overseas' soldiers, the production process involves many skilled personnel being directed within a business and its suppliers by a hierarchy or managerial authority, supported by the self-regulations of trade practices across the chartered professions, such as accountancy and engineering. The function of this defence firm is to manufacture this tank by bringing together a series of designers, suppliers, production, and distribution operations: indeed, a long-held convention by many economists is that the key advantage of organizing production and distribution through businesses is that it involves lower transaction costs through the dynamics of manufacturing specialization, the repeat processes of production, innovation and targeted marketing.[6] The ***function*** of this mythical tank manufacturer is not to export per se, but to organize, resource and produce materials and equipment effectively, efficiently, and economically.

The ***purpose*** of the business, however, is different from its function. According to conventional economic wisdom, the aim is to maximize profits thereby offering the best returns to investors.[7] For a UK defence business, William Foulds, the managing director of Redstone Risk, argues that:[8]

> The functions of a normal defence firm are symbiotic with the way it is organised and goes about its business. The goal is to maximise the profits that can be made following significant shareholder and other investments. This means maximising market penetration: overseas' sales, therefore, typically become a matter of priority for defence boards of directors.

Defence exports, in other words, should not necessarily be viewed as artefacts of a nation's geopolitical ambition. Rather, they are a product of the normal rules of economics: if the unit price offers a profit after all costs are considered, the more a company sells of a tank, plane or weapons' system, the more money it makes – meeting the goals of the business. A board's search for exports is simply a desire for enhanced market penetration thereby maximizing the returns that can be offered to the owners. Under this analysis, the defence company, along with the sector as a whole, at its kernel follows the norms and practices of the free market. There are no special conditions linked to defence.

This argument could be taken even further. BAE Systems, for instance, announced its end-of-year results for Financial Year 2021 on 24 February 2022. Sales of £21.3 billion over the year had generated profits before interest and tax of £2.2 billion. This was consistent with results from earlier years, despite the pandemic and before the business effects of the war in Ukraine were to be felt. As Charles Woodburn, the chief executive of the Group stated:[9]

> Our diverse portfolio, together with our focus on programme execution, cash generation and efficiencies..[mean].. we are well positioned for sustained top line and margin growth in the coming years.

The end-of-year report was presented to the City through the prism of the various business divisions within BAE Systems: the Electronic Systems business; Platforms and Services in the United States; the Air and Maritime businesses; and the cyber and intelligence divisions, one centred in the United States and the other in the United Kingdom. Exports from the United Kingdom were embedded in the Report[10] under these divisions, not exposed separately, suggesting that overseas' sales were routine and integrated undertakings – normal business, in other words, not the result of specific British Government-BAE Systems' geopolitical campaigns executing British government policy.

Notable exports highlighted through the 2021 results were the 24 Typhoon and nine Hawk aircraft, support and training contracts being delivered to Qatar. A contract to Kuwait for further Typhoon aircraft was mentioned also as progressing well, along with a £1.3 billion order from the German Air Force for 38 Typhoon aircraft, replacing those currently in service.

Special mention was made of Saudi Arabia and Australia, with both being treated as core, home markets for BAE Systems. The same was true for the United States, where:[11]

> The US continues to represent the world's largest defence budget and accounts for around 46 percent of our revenues.

Given that the United States is BAE Systems' largest market serviced through, principally, the company's division located in the country, an analyst could speculate whether BAE Systems is a British company at all, irrespective of where its shares are traded of where the group headquarters is located. With such a complex, global, interdependent business, the very idea of exports from a place to a place might even be outdated.

The company itself would argue that it provides advanced, technology-led defence, aerospace and security solutions to the West and its partners, through a workforce of 90,500 people employed in 40 countries. It is international by design and deliberate corporate strategy.[12] This allows the company to invest in advanced, technological research and development as innovations and insights through research benefit and span a group-wide portfolio of revenues and programmes.[13] This work comes on to discuss research and development in a future chapter, but for now it is important to acknowledge the criticality of technology development to the defence business.

A Different Purpose? The Defence Business and the Environment

A premise of this chapter is that the purpose of a defence business is to maximize profits through the hidden-hand manifestations of the free market. Therefore, a corporate ambition for overseas' sales of defence equipment is merely one manifestation of this commercial ambition. It is worth reflecting, though, whether a UK defence business could articulate other goals, perhaps matched to an underlying profit motive. Let us consider the defence sector's response to the climate change agenda, in this regard.

A significant revision to the Climate Change Act of 2008, passed by Parliament in June 2019, required the UK Government to reduce the Kingdom's net emissions of greenhouse gases by 100 percent (relative to 1990 levels) by 2050, thereby becoming a net zero emitter.[14] This legislative commitment accords with the 2016 Paris Agreement to keep global warming to under two degrees Celsius. The Act and Agreement both recognize and assert that, for humanity, climate change is an existential threat. Consequently, it has been said that Britain and Northern Ireland should lead efforts to interdict the effects of climate change, especially as the country contributed historically to the generation of greenhouse gases through UK primacy in the industrial revolution.[15]

Beyond treaty and legislative obligations, and a political aspiration for leadership of the climate change risk management agenda as part of Global Britain,[16] reaching net zero is said to have important strategic socio-economic benefits for the United Kingdom:

- On the assumption that it is achieved with international partners and peers, the existential threat to the natural environment, global built communities and 21st century ways of living substantially reduces, though the methods of calculating the value of that reduction and the benefits incurred are contested;[17]
- Human health is improved as a result of better air quality, temperature distribution, a protected natural ecosystem and built environment that takes account of climate change risk mitigations in build design, materials used and steady-state resource consumption. Hospital admissions, as a consequence, are reduced substantially and social security costs are shrunk. Economic productivity is modelled to improve through the

consequences of better health and social care outcomes and the cumulative effects of sustainable environmental policies and practices.

The costs of achieving this prize of net zero are estimated at being somewhere between £50 and £70 billion per annum, or in excess of £1 trillion (at 2020 values) by 2050. Whilst a substantial sum, the Committee on Climate Change predicts that the economic value of productivity and quality of life benefits is equal to the costs associated with the risk management of climate change.[18]

Of course, these values and projections need to be treated with caution. The underlying economic assumptions can change as new challenges (managing a coherent and effective Covid-19 response, for instance), technologies and practices emerge. For example, the costs of offshore wind generation fell by over a third in 2019 alone, making predictions foolhardy around the long-term utility, or otherwise, of this technology. The underlying message, though, remains clear: left unchecked, climate change is an existential threat. Governments around the world are seeking treaty agreements, legislating within their own borders and setting policy obligations on their institutions and peoples, to interdict and reverse the strategic dangers of its impact.[19] In the case of the United Kingdom, this is a whole of government imperative and, as William Hague states:[20]

> … [the] transition to net zero requires perhaps the fastest and most complete change to human society ever brought about in a peaceful democracy.

Defence businesses that operate in the United Kingdom, and the MoD in particular, cannot be exempt from this endeavour. Rather, the Department:[21]

> Must act now to seize the opportunity to respond to the impact of climate change on future operational effectiveness, sustainability, resilience and security at home and abroad. As a major military power, defence's leadership in building security, adapting to the climate changed world and reducing emissions should be at the forefront of the Government's ambition for the Green Industrial Revolution.

There is a hard edge to the possible contribution of defence. Whilst the MoD, as a major government department, must embrace government policy on emissions' reductions, the clear-eyed imperative is to ensure that the armed forces can continue to operate, survive and thrive in a period *either* of accelerating climate change *or* in an environment embracing the technological innovations and working practices designed to interdict the effects of these changes. The consequences for UK defence decision-makers are, clearly, profound.

At one level of analysis, the case for overt investments to interdict the effects of climate change, and to promote the generation of sustainable defence capabilities, seems strong – and this argument appears to flow across all Defence lines of development (DLOD)[22]. With the equipment DLOD, for example, by 2050 fossil-fuel-based power solutions should be, pretty much, obsolete, the preserve of legacy platforms. Any new or emerging Defence solution between now and then, relying on traditional fuels, has the potential to become an expensive white elephant. Under this scenario, companies will be contracted by the MoD or a prime contractor to manufacture engines based on 2020 (and earlier) technology at a time when commercial research and development investments and facilities have focussed businesses on alternative power packages. Historical, niche preferences over the technological solutions of 'now' invariably attract a cost premium.[23] Therefore, investing in the development of alternative power solutions not only offers climate change mitigation benefits to Defence (and society), but suggests long-term budgetary benefits also. Naturally, such technologies and refreshed ways-of-working would be attractive to export markets.

With training, a second DLOD, and a significant component of annual Defence expenditure, there are also challenges to overcome. For example, climate change is causing the loss of seven to ten training days in Cyprus per annum, with projections showing that, in a short time, the whole of August might be lost each year to the military training schedulers.[24] This will mean that more reliance is placed on the Defence Training Estate in the United Kingdom with blended training and simulation becoming more significant.

In this regard, the efficiency and durability of UK-based training, the estate it is conducted upon and the attainment of proven, reliable non-fossil-fuel-based power solutions become important indicators of Defence's ability to meet CC&S contributions whilst concurrently generating critical defence capabilities. A focus on the defence training estate, therefore, might prove an important access point into a proactive and productive emerging CC&S strategy for Defence. As Lt. Gen Nugee, MoD's CC&S non-executive director, told the author:[25]

> … for me, this is a revolutionary moment in our capability generation, not evolutionary business as usual.

Such a focus would build upon extant MoD-commercial partnerships that have generated benefits already. Effective, 'gain-shared' public–private working is, perhaps, the standard required for future contracting for support to the Defence Training Estate, and the whole of the UK defence sector more broadly, out to 2050.

For example, the DIO, its industry partner, Landmarc Support Services, and the modular construction specialist, Reds 10, have worked together as an integrated project team to provide affordable and carbon-efficient accommodation across the Defence Training Estate. This was part of a £45 million net-zero carbon accommodation programme that began in January 2020. The first phase of the project provided 18 new accommodation blocks with a further 22 buildings planned for delivery during Phase Two.

The building prototype at Westdown Camp yielded an Energy Performance Certificate (EPC) of 12 points from carbon neutral, delivered, principally, through the use of air service heat pumps and roof-top solar panels as sources of energy. Lessons identified from continual data analyses of the Westdown Camp site offered the opportunity to redesign and reconfigure elements of the modular construction solution so that the next units, constructed for the Nesscliff Training Area, had a negative EPC certification – MoD was, effectively, selling energy back to the national grid. To date, this programme has seen a total reduction in embodied carbon of approximately 130 tonnes, and hints at a broader contribution, through the defence training estate, that Defence could make to CC&S mitigation and national resilience without any risk to the degradation of capabilities – quite the opposite, in fact.

This programme offers some important considerations that need drawing out:

- It is an exemplar public–private endeavour, sharing risks, collectively innovating and committed to a military end-user through principles of modularity, flexibility, affordability and continuous learning;
- The programme was deliberately phased and financed so that the lessons and understandings gleaned from earlier activities in the schedule could influence latter initiatives;
- Data analytics, modelling and regular performance and design reviews are critical to this way of working, and;
- It presents as an understandable example of the confluence of smart thinking around future capability generation and necessary action towards CC&S mitigation, easily explained to decision-makers and Service users alike, with lessons applicable to other Defence activities.
- A relationship between the MoD and a UK business focussed on the national estate offers significant export opportunities for the company as it seeks to exploit the knowledge generated from its climate change activities in the United Kingdom.

Landmarc Support Services was contracted to undertake the development of carbon-neutral facilities for use on the defence estate. Its managing director, Mark Neill suggested that:[26]

> The long-term contract we have with the MoD allows us to help them with the broader problems faced by UK defence, such as climate change. Defence businesses need to make a profit but that is not the only motivation. We want to do the right thing by our UK client and export great learning and best practices to the UK's allies when we can.

The case for the defence business in the United Kingdom is more nuanced, perhaps, then simply making money. Also, the imperative for exports in maximizing profits is rooted in learning generated from UK contracts between MoD and onshore businesses. Monies spent by the MoD with UK businesses on national requirements seemingly allow the UK corporation to generate products and services to export to the country's allies. It seems that, on occasions, there is a symbiotic relationship between the UK Government and its defence businesses that are not merely commercial in design and execution.

The Defence Enterprise

Accepting this significant nuance in interpretation, a major premise of this chapter is that defence exports from the United Kingdom are simply an articulation of normal and sound business practices of the firms concerned. As a consequence, such exports cannot, of themselves, be draped in geopolitical significance, as an extension, for instance, of British defence and security policies. Indeed, as seen with BAE Systems, it becomes challenging to conceive of the company as solely British when its range of diverse activities, programmes and sources of revenues are explored. The Board of BAE Systems develops its own strategies to exploit its opportunities and minimize its risks, and those strategies are unique and bespoke to BAE Systems. Do such companies, headquarters in the United Kingdom, however, really travel alone? Could there be, perhaps, a range of interdependencies, customer obligations and supply-chain components more akin to an economic and social ecosystem for the defence sector that constrains and shapes the actions of such companies?[27] It might well be that BAE Systems should be perceived as a node of a rather complex and constantly shape-shifting public-private enterprise rather than a stand-alone commercial entity, developing export plans at will.

In 2015, scholars introduced the concept of the 'defence extended enterprise,' exploring the idea of defence companies sitting in a 'cat's cradle' of public–private elements that, together, formed an amorphous, though observable, defence enterprise.[28] The essence of this concept was the hypothesis that the British Government failed to understand properly the significance of its supply base for defence and security purposes, onshore and internationally. The government, therefore, accepted risks, uncertainties and unknowns that should have been mitigated to keep the UK population as safe as possible. The defence business was a critical component of a cross-border and internal network of people, know-how, technologies (known and emerging) and materials that, together, at the point of integration, offered the United Kingdom its capacity for undertaking defence missions. Moreover, different businesses could come and go in different shapes, sizes and identities, tied-together at a specific moment through various defence contracts. The constant, though, was the defence enterprise itself which, like all ecosystems, has to be constantly fed and refreshed.[29]

The desire and ability to sell defence products overseas was simply an exercise in sustaining the business within the defence enterprise through increased market share, cash injections and profits which, in turn, satisfied investors and other sources of capital. Defence exports, consequently, are a critical component of the defence enterprise, central to its health and well-being in the United Kingdom. For the government and MoD in particular:[30]

> It is not enough to simply recognise the existence of the extended enterprise. There is a need also actively to manage it by anticipating the future; giving direction, and planning, organising, coordinating and monitoring performance.

Conclusion

This chapter started with the notion of the British defence business being 'merchants of death,' echoing the stance taken by some of those who view defence exports through an ethical prism only. This idea, though powerful and persuasive, as the review and analysis in Chapter 2 outlined, was countered, in part, by defence sector employees themselves: the people of Barrow, for instance, did not see themselves as architects of mayhem and destruction. The chapter went on to place the defence businesses that export weapons and support capabilities simply in a narrative of commercial best practice, with defence business executives seeking overseas' sales to boost top-line and profit imperatives. In this regard, the defence business, was like any commercial entity that seeks to maximize turnover and returns to investors. In the case of BAE Systems, also, doing so contributed to the employment of 91,000 people in the United Kingdom and around the world, before supply chains were included. Whilst with BAE Systems, the point was made that the global nature of the group, its diverse governmental customers and production domains, made it difficult to conceptualize as just 'British.' This is a theme to which we return when defence exports as technology transfers is considered.

There was a sense, also, that whilst the commercial drivers for business executives could be understood, and defence exports normalized in this context, profit was not the only motivation for defence businesses. As the section on climate change suggested, business contribution to factors other than the production of weapons, for example, can be identified and might be significant to a broader UK policy agenda. Also, the learning gleaned in the United Kingdom, potentially, can be packaged and exported to Britain's allies.

Lastly, the thought was offered that defence businesses in the United Kingdom are not merely isolated commercial actors, guided by the hidden-hand of supply and demand imperatives, but rather nodes and components of a more complex defence-extended enterprise. For this enterprise to be successful, the government was needed to both compose the music and conduct the orchestra of public and commercial players. How successfully this is being done is considered in the following chapters.

Notes

1 Lauren Twort and Gabriela Thompson, 'The Twenty-First Century Armoury: A Town Called Barrow,' in *The RUSI Journal,* 2017, p. 4. DOI: 10.1080/03071847.2017.1380336.
2 The 'C-Suite' refers to the company's chiefs' suite of offices. The executive directors of a business such as Chief Executive, Chief Operating Officer, Chief Finance Officer and so on.
3 Richard L. Daft, *Organizational Theory and Design* (New York, NY: West Publishing Company, 1995) p. 9.
4 Ibid.
5 Maritza van de Heuvel, Joanne Ho and Jim Benson, *Beyond Agile: Tales of Continuous Improvement* (Seattle, WA: Modus Cooperandi Press, 2013).
6 Ronald H. Coase, 'The Nature of the Firm,' in *Economica,* 1937, Vol. 4, No. 16, pp. 386–405.
7 John Sloman, Kevin Hinde and Dean Garratt, *Economics for Business* (Harlow: Pearson, 2013) p. 13.
8 William Foulds, speaking with the author on 25th April 2022, in Exeter.
9 www.baesystems.com accessed on 24th February 2022.
10 BAE Systems Preliminary Announcement 2021, https://investors.baesystems.com/~/media/Files/B/Bae-Systems-Investor-Relations-V3/PDFs/results-and-reports/results/2022/2021-preliminary-results-announcement.pdf
11 Ibid., p. 10.
12 Ibid., p. 6.
13 Ibid., pp. 9–10.
14 The Climate Change Act 2008 (2050 Target Amendment) Order 2019, at www.legislation.gov.uk/uksi/2029/1056/contents/made.
15 Michael Gove, 'the industrial revolution means the UK has a moral responsibility to lead on climate change,' (12 February 2020), Carbon Brief Daily Briefing at www.carbonbrief.org/daily-brief.
16 House of Commons Library, *Research Briefing: Global Britain* (London: HoC, 6 January 2021).
17 The Institute for Government, *UK Net Zero Target*, 20 April 2020 at www.instituteforgovernment.org.uk.
18 The Committee on Climate Change, *Net Zero: the UK's Contribution to Stopping Global Warming*, 2 May 2019 at www.theccc.org.uk/publications.
19 The Institute for Government, *UK Net Zero Target*, 20 April 2020 at www.instituteforgovernment.org.uk.
20 William Hague, 'PM must level with us if he wants to level up,' in *The Times*, Tuesday June 15 2021.
21 Lt Gen Richard Nugee, *Climate Change and Sustainability Report* (London: MoD, 18 December 2018) p. 6.
22 In the UK, Defence lines of development are Training, Equipment, People, Information, Doctrine, Organisations, Infrastructure, Logistics and Integration.
23 Per Lundin, Niklas Stenlas and Johan Gribbe (Eds), *Science for Welfare and Warfare: Technology and State Initiative in Cold War Sweden* (Sagamore Beach, MA: Watson Publishing International, 2010).
24 Interview with Lt Gen Richard Nugee, 5th July 2021.

25 Ibid.
26 Interview with Mark Neill, 24th February 2022.
27 James E. Post, Lee E, Preston and Sybille Sachs, 'Managing the Extended Enterprise: The New Stakeholder View,' in *California Management Review*, Vol 45, No. 1, Fall 2002.
28 John Louth and Trevor Taylor, 'Beyond the Whole Force: The Concept of the Defence Extended Enterprise and Its Implications for the Ministry of Defence,' *RUSI Occasional Paper, 2015* (London: RUSI, 2015).
29 Andrew Humphries and Richard Gibbs, *Enterprise Relationship Management: A Paradigm for Alliance Success* (Farnham: Gower, 2015.)
30 Louth and Taylor, p. 7.

6 Defence Exports and International Development

Introduction

When an overseas' government purchases defence weapons, know-how or support services from the British, it does so, typically, to achieve three things. First, an increase in its own military capabilities. Second, an improved within-border knowledge through the transfer of industrial capacity, especially technologies and design and build competencies. Third, an enhanced relationship with the British Government and the UK defence business in question. Also, by providing British-assured defence capabilities to partner nations, the United Kingdom will meet, potentially, one of the strands of its self-heralded international development strategy, published in May 2022, whereby the British will[1]

> … help countries escape cycles of conflict and violence which underpin so many protracted humanitarian emergencies and in which malign actors can advance their interests.

The premise of this chapter, therefore, is that British defence exports contribute towards the development of partner nations. In exploring this hypothesis, at the outset, we consider further the notions of defence exports' offsets, a concept most associated with client-state development. The chapter goes on to explore peer-state development, with countries such as those in NATO or the 5-Eyes Alliance. Also considered, are near-peer developing nations, and we consider a specific case from the continent of Africa. Thereafter, the conflict in Ukraine is explored as an extreme example of defence export aid seeking to help in the development of Ukraine's responses to Russian aggression and invasion in 2022.

Lastly, the chapter reviews the premise that, whilst defence exports from the United Kingdom might contribute to a client nation's development, that development of itself might not be altogether positive, or lead to outcomes that the British themselves – politician and citizen – might find unacceptable.

It is important at the outset, however, to note that development, as a topic, is interwoven with notions of the application and exploitation of

DOI: 10.4324/9781003221494-6

emerging technologies: development, after all, is about providing a partner or client-state with capabilities and enabling competencies that it seeks to possess but, currently, struggles to access. History suggests that great powers continue to adopt new technologies to defence and security uses, and that secondary and emerging powers will seek to imitate them. This can take the form of the acquisition of advanced weaponry or enabling systems from a leading power, the development of the client-state's own industrial base to generate such systems, through the practices of offsets, or both. Development, therefore, might not be about simply offering client and emerging states an entry point into today's advance military technologies. Rather, the subject might be concerned with providing pathways into tomorrow's advanced technological defence systems: development reconfigured as military proliferation, perhaps, of the future, technology-rich components of tomorrow's battlefield. Such a scenario could represent a truly revolutionary moment in human history:[2]

> Along with the military utilisation of artificial intelligence and autonomous weapons, the transformative role of emerging technologies is also evident in the development of a wide array of hypersonic missiles and directed-energy systems.

The UK commitment to the development of its allies through defence exports might be viewed, by tomorrow's historians, as a 'gateway drug' into ever more lethal and dangerous defence technologies, with their future proliferation linked to a UK national policy of international development.

Offsets as Development

The notion of 'offsets' was introduced briefly in an earlier chapter but the concept is most associated with defence exports and their contribution towards a purchasing nation's economic and social development. With offsets, there are two commercial transactions. The first is the trade in defence materials themselves: the British defence company, for instance, sells weapons or support services to specification and the importing nation pays the fees agreed in the contract. This can be straight to the business, known as a direct sale, or via the British Government under a government-to-government contract. An example of the latter is the Al Yamamah arms deal between BAE Systems, Saudi Arabia and the British Government, introduced in Chapter 1, where aircraft were provided to Saudi Arabia from BAE Systems, the Saudis paid the British Government in oil, and that government settled the monies owed to BAE Systems in hard currency.

The second transaction is the accompanying offset deal itself. The exporting company agrees to invest in the purchasing country to 'offset' the cost of the arms' purchased. In this manner, classically, the export is said to assist in the economic and social development of the purchasing nation. To push the point further, defence sales to emerging powers – in the Middle East, for instance – suggests that UK businesses could be viewed as executing, in part, the British Government's international development agenda.

Historically, the global demand for offset by purchasing countries has been driven by four, interlocking, factors:[3]

- The size and value of the defence export drives the scale and quality of the offset package demanded;
- The ability of the procuring country to absorb and generate benefits from the offsets being offered;
- The flexibility and accessibility of the offset policy of the procuring nation and its attractiveness and acceptability to the vendor; and
- The commitment, or otherwise, of the importing nation to its own offset policy, especially where it has been seen to fail with other, earlier programmes.

Even if these four factors are settled to the mutual satisfaction of the importing nation, the vender, and its home government, there can still be challenges. For, offset:[4]

> … embraces not only local military platform manufacturers, but also the broader ecosystem embracing 'dual-use' technologies, R&D institutions, innovative supply chains, frontier engineering universities and the abundance of highly skilled scientists, technician and engineers. In theory, most offset will be stillborn in the absence of viable absorptive capacity.

An additional problem with offset transactions, of course, is the potential for corruption, given the vast sums of money typically moving between multiple jurisdictions. As we saw earlier in the book, the Al Yamamah deal has attracted significant accusations of bribery, illegal payments and substantial, unlawful, benefits in kind to Saudi Arabian officials from UK-based defence businesses.

Peer-State Development

At a peer-state level, the exporting of defence ideas, materials and know-how for the military and industrial development of a friendly state is often wrapped up in notions around international collaboration. It is important to note, however, that there is a difference between *international collaboration* involving Great Britain and *defence exports* from the United Kingdom. The latter, as discussed earlier in this work, is where a specific product or service is purchased and exported under state-sponsored export controls. The former, in contrast, exists where two or more states come together to agree to work collaboratively on the development and production of a defence system that meets mutual military needs. In this manner, duplication of effort is said to be reduced and the concentration of resources supposedly leads to quicker in-service timelines. Typical components of collaborative programmes are their expense, and the unaffordability of states to 'go it alone,' the potential for exports to countries beyond the initial partners yielding much-needed revenues, and the generation of workshare for onshore, nationally located defence companies.[5] The development of the Lockheed-Martin led F-35 combat air programme is an example of such a multi-state collaboration.

However, a number of collaborative programmes have been criticized over the years. Analysts have pointed to the potential for excessive transaction costs, associated with internal markets and enhanced transfer prices generated by the collaborative partners. The governmental and industrial elements of a programme, and their respective supply chains, typically give rise to an inflexible programme bureaucracy and management by political consensus, driving inefficiencies and bad decision-making. This has led to delays in delivery, expensive rework and cost growth. Indeed, the UK National Audit Office has calculated that total development costs on collaborative defence programmes and projects were between 140 and 200 percent higher than for comparable national programmes, depending upon the number of partners involved.[6]

Possibly, the most high-profile collaborative programmes over the next few decades will be those associated with future combat air systems. In the case of the United Kingdom, the Government has teamed with Italy, Sweden, and Japan to develop Tempest, a sixth-generation fighter jet expected to enter service in 2035. The principal defence industrial partners are BAE Systems, Rolls-Royce, Leonardo and MBDA. Over the life of this defence system, the total costs estimated by the UK's Infrastructure and Project Authority are £72 billion.[7]

> The Tempest is supposed to be faster, stealthier and cleverer than any previous fighter jet ... the aircraft will be studded with sensors from nose to tail and these will gather a "spider's web" of data. This will be knitted together and analysed by a lightning-fast brain ... It's a flying supercomputer.

Using advanced technologies and virtual worlds, it is said that the pilot will have a host of weapons to choose from or the option to act as a node in a super-information or intelligence highway.

The point of such collaborative programmes as these is that governments and businesses are developing future systems based on a blend of known and emerging technologies and novel components. In the Tempest case, for instance, the ambition is to generate an engine where the fuel burns at a hotter temperature than the melting point of its components, bending the laws of physics to the will of the programme. The Japanese and Swedish nations and their domestic industries, no doubt, will benefit from the development of Tempest, but this is a byproduct of the programme's intent. The British are not exporting defence equipment and technology to develop peer partners through such a programme. Rather, those partners are best perceived as end-users, customers and sources of finance.

This is not the case with the Hunter frigate programme in Australia, for example, which is a blend of British defence export and developmental collaboration. The Strategic Defence and Security Review of 2010 (SDSR 2010) announced the establishment of the future frigate programme to replace the ageing Type 23 ships of the Royal Navy. The new ships were to be known as the Type 26 Class, to be built by BAE Systems, with the first to be HMS Glasgow. Following a formal competition in Australia, in 2016 the Australian Government announced that it had chosen the Type 26 design as the basis of its next-generation anti-submarine ship,[8] to be known at the Hunter Class.[9]

> For the UK, this was a success for governmental and marketing sales effort dating back more than five years as well as a tribute to the capabilities expected of the ship.

Whilst a commercial success for BAE Systems, the Hunter programme represents the export of strategic capabilities from the United Kingdom to Australia. It is an enabler of military and industrial development.

In Australia, programmes such as Hunter are recapitalizing the defence industrial base with personnel and know-how relocating from the United Kingdom to defence clusters around cities such as Adelaide, for instance. Without the British core design and transferable engineering and technology competencies, the growth of this key element of Australian defence and security capability would, potentially, stall.

Instead, rather than driving costs and inefficiencies, targeted programme collaborations following a successful export, offer the opportunity for doctrinal, operational, and through-life support convergence. This, in turn, would need to sit on a cat's-cradle of essential, critical technologies and digital pathways of working. The potential convergence between these two national programmes, therefore, offers substantial benefits of economies of scale, joint learning and knowledge harvesting, pooling and sharing, potentially, through notions of strategic fleet reserves and efficiencies that might not be available to solely national programmes in the 21st century. The development of Australian capabilities through this strategic defence export, in other words, also has the potential to enhance Britain's own upgrade of its frigate fleet.

If defence as a sector is, as this book argues, a multi-faceted ecosystem where critical competencies, capacity, mass, technologies and capital reside in the commercial sector, often off-shore and international, both by nature and design, there is an added degree of difficulty to the generation of national defence capabilities that convergence and collaboration might address. In the case of the Australian requirement, this potential starts with Britain's commitment to assist in the development, through exports, of Australian maritime capabilities. The significance of this cannot be understated.

This work returns to the Glasgow-Hunter programme(s) within both the chapters on partnering and research and development. For now, though, we consider development through defence exports in near-peer states.

British Defence Exports and the Developing World

Of course, international development is understood typically in the context of the developing world and its emerging powers rather than peer-states to Britain such as Australia in the case above. In this regard, the United Kingdom has a history of exporting defence systems and dual-use technologies to developing countries and emerging powers. These contracts and arrangements are not normally of the scale of a Type 26 frigate or Tempest future aircraft proposition, with the exception, of course, of contracts with the Gulf monarchies. The British Government's incentive for exporting defence goods and services to developing nations is probably as follows:[10]

- Enhancing the security and protection of existing or emerging allies;
- Constraining the political and commercial activities of allies, binding the recipient nation to the UK strategic interest;
- Using the prospect of defence transfers as leverage over the domestic government's internal and external behaviour;
- Creating the economies of scale, possibly by 'baby steps,' to sustain the onshore British defence industrial and technological base; and
- Developing the infrastructure, technical know-how and capacity of the recipient nation.

This final notion of inward development of emerging powers through defence imports from the United Kingdom does not stand alone, somehow apart from the other incentives. Rather, for developing nations, imported defence capabilities are linked to ideas of prestige, domestic safety, resilience and the building of strategic allegiances:[11]

> For example, Gulf Arab monarchies undertake arms purchases ... to create links that will guarantee protection for their regimes.

Also, in emerging and developing world polities, there does appear to be an empirical link between expenditure on defence imports, economic growth and broader social benefits such as training, employment opportunities and improvements in indigenous repair, maintenance, and overhaul capabilities.[12]

Notwithstanding this, there are significant challenges associated with defence exports from Britain to the developing world. In the early years of the 21st century, the country of Tanzania, for example, was 151st on the list of the UN's Human Development Index – out of 173 nation-states. By any standard, it was one of the poorest countries in the world. Its leaders decided that, to aid its development, a key acquisition would be a military-grade air traffic control system. It is alleged that this decision, in part, was influenced by the then British prime minister, Tony Blair, who had established a Commission for Africa as a UK contribution to the development of countries on that continent.[13]

> Tony Blair persuaded the President of Tanzania, one of the world's poorest countries, to purchase an air radar system for military aircraft at a cost of over $40 million. At the time Tanzania had an air force of eight planes, most of which were in various states of disrepair.

Some analysts might argue that one of the last things an impoverished country with a negligible air force required is a military-level air traffic control system. The Tanzanian authorities argued at the time, and subsequently, that their requirement was for a primary civil aviation control system with an option for occasional military use as the country developed and in the future re-capitalized its military aviation. BAE Systems, in 2001, was contracted to provide the Watchman system, a major air force asset usually associated with first-world military capabilities. The UN International Civil Aviation Organization (ICAO) thought the deal ridiculous:[14]

> The system as contracted is primarily a military system and can provide limited support to civil air traffic control purposes. The purchase of additional equipment ... would be required to render it useful for civil air traffic control. However, if it is to be used primarily for civil air traffic control purposes, the proposed system is not adequate and too expensive.

For the ICAO, the system purchased did not meet the requirement set of primary civil aviation control with occasional usage by the military. The World Bank also questioned the folly of the deal, observing that $40 million was, at the time, a third of the resources committed in Tanzania towards basic national education.[15] Speculation was to emerge that bribes of almost £10 million were allegedly paid to ensure the contract was awarded.[16]

In this regard, it should be noted that BAE Systems inherited the emerging deal with the Tanzanian Government when the company bought Siemens Plessey Systems in 1997. The latter business had been negotiating a deal for the sale of radar and support equipment for a number of years ahead of the takeover. As part of the transaction, Siemens Plessey transferred the company's in-country agent to BAE Systems. As argued in Chapter 2, a key structural source of, and conduit for, corrupt practices is the defence sector's practice of using agents to execute transactions in country ahead of contracts being awarded. Many agents operate ethically, within the laws of the country concerned and the international community. Business development, though, can bleed into bribes in the hands of the corrupt and unethical. In the Tanzanian case, speculation continues, of course, but an international warrant was issued for the arrest of the agent in 2007.[17] Moreover,[18]

> The vast majority of corruption cases in the arms trade … involve third-party agents or intermediaries, through whom bribes are typically channelled to their final recipients.

As this book has argued, it does seem significant that a total of 31 out of 35 arms trade cases in the World Peace Foundation's Compendium of Arms Trade Corruption involve such figures playing senior roles in unethical and illegal activities in support of the pursuit of contract award.[19] That, in the case of Tanzania, the contract was framed as development assistance is especially concerning.

The Case of Ukraine: Survival Not Development

In this decade, analysts have been forced to consider issues where defence exports for the development of a British ally or client-state have morphed into the export of defence materials to assist in the very survival of the state. Such a case, of course, is Ukraine. On 24 February 2022, Russia initiated a full-scale invasion of the country to recover, in part, its European sphere of influence and control. The response of the British Government was to condemn the Russian leadership's 'unprovoked and premeditated war against Ukraine.'[20] The UK's defence export regime was utilized to offer capabilities not for the long-term military and economic development of an allied state, but for its immediate, short-term survival. As the British Government stated

> The UK and our international partners are united in support for Ukraine. The UK government is providing a range of economic, humanitarian and defensive military assistance to Ukraine, and imposing sanctions on Russia and Belarus.

The choice of words within this official Government statement is interesting. On the modern battlefield, it is difficult to discern between offensive and defensive capabilities thereby making the notion of just providing defensive assistance fairly meaningless: lethality is lethality. Rather, the United Kingdom is providing substantial military material and training to the Ukrainians in their fight. They are defending their homeland through offensive operations against the invader using, as part of the armoury,

The Multiple Launch Rocket System (M270) And Munitions (M31A1)
In excess of 5,000 NLAW anti-tank missiles
More than 200 Javelin anti-tank missiles
120 armoured personnel vehicles
1,360 ant-structure munitions
5 air defence systems including Starstreak missiles
4.5 tonnes of plastic explosive
Stormer vehicles fitted with launchers for anti-air missiles
New anti-ship missile systems
More than 400,000 rounds of small arms ammunition
In excess of 200,000 pieces of non-lethal aid such as helmets and body armour.
Electronic warfare equipment
Counter battery radar systems
GPS jamming equipment
Thousands of night vision devices
Heavy lift UAV systems to provide logistics support to isolated forces
Over 20 M109 155mm artillery guns

MILITARY EQUIPMENT EXPORTED FROM THE UK TO UKRAINE

Figure 6.1 UK Defence Equipment Exports to Ukraine.

Source: House of Commons.

British-provided military systems. Indeed, Figure 6.1 identifies the equipment provided by the United Kingdom as of the summer of 2022. It is stretching logic too far to describe the packages as 'defensive' in nature.

Defence exports, therefore, can be cloaked in a narrative of economic and social development, the resilience of a client-state and a defensive posture, but their lethal utility is always a fundamental element of the proposition. This should offer us no surprises. Using defence materials to help allies develop and respond to challenges and threats, for the United Kingdom, has been always about the development of enduring relationships and Britain's reputation and place in the world. Championing Western support for Ukraine allows the British leadership an opportunity to assert its role in Europe, post-Brexit, and to restate its belief in NATO in Europe as a cornerstone of the continent's security.[21] The active and continuing arming of Ukraine affords the British an opportunity to avoid a future whereby:[22]

> The world is no longer so liberal democratic nor so ordered that a mid-rank democratic power can look after itself, still less pursue … elevated global aspirations.

The protection and development of others through defence exports, after all, might be about, in equal measure, the development and promotion of the British themselves in a changing and confusing world order. Should this be correct, defence exports from the United Kingdom provided under the banner of development, might be multi-faceted, performing a myriad of functions – the very hypothesis of this book, in fact.

To Celebrate or Condemn? Development Through Defence Exports

Working backwards through this chapter, it seems reasonable, even noble, for the British authorities and people to support Ukraine in the face of ruthless aggression. That the battle for Ukraine is an existential moment for that country seems obvious and at the time the danger clear and present. The use of defence exports from the United Kingdom as a policy response for the British speaks to their importance as a security option – to both the immediate defence of the state and then its economic and security development, post-conflict. An early judgement must be that military exports are positive and to be welcomed in a case such as Ukraine.

The case of Tanzania is more challenging and disturbing. The charge sheet seems to be that British industry, championed by the Blair Government, sold the Tanzanian authorities a military system that was not fit for the purposes (mostly civil air traffic control) for which it was procured. Whilst 'let the buyer beware' is a cornerstone of English commercial law, Tanzania was a poor, developing state that could scarcely afford the contract terms, given the demands placed on the national exchequer for health, education, and other critical investments. The sense that the British were able to secure this contract through the nefarious activities of a national agent allegedly offering bribes, adds to this sense of discomfort. Indeed, the UK Secretary of State for International Development, Clare Short, said at the time that[23]

> The thing was so grubby from beginning to end and, of course, it was so old that the technology was overtaken. Tanzania didn't have military aircraft. It needed civil air traffic control improvements in order to improve its tourist industry.

It seems reasonable that analyst and citizen alike would condemn both the content of the Tanzanian deal and the manner in which it was executed. It represents a failure of British Government policy and ethics.

Conclusion

This chapter has sought to demonstrate that British policy is rich in the discourse of international development, framed as a set of tools, techniques and interventions to enable countries (mostly in the developing world) to escape conflict, violence and economic underperformance.[24] The case has been made that defence exports from the United Kingdom is one element of the toolbox charged with enabling targeted developmental outcomes. Counterintuitively, the defence export itself can be between either peer states, as in the case of the UK–Australian relationship cited as an example, or with client/developing states seeking to take advantage of the UK's supposedly greater technology and know-how.

There seems an inherent contradiction here. Most readers would object to a first-world country like Australia, somehow, being 'developed' through defence exports in the same manner as a state such as Tanzania. But the reality, of course, is that the Australians needed British design, development and manufacturing competencies to recapitalize decaying maritime capacities. The export of the Type 26 class has to be seen, in part, through this lens.

The development of Tanzania through the export of a military air traffic control system was also about development, its advocates would suggest. That this deal seems mired in corruption and scandal is hard to contest and the roles of offsets and national agents open to substantial criticism. The monies associated with defence exports seemingly attract the corrupt: a double-whammy where these very programmes supposedly aid development and counter governmental and societal corruption rather than enable and institutionalize such practices. The Tanzania case also raises questions around the effectiveness and durability of the British defence exports' approvals process. Moreover, for UK policymakers, could it be that British jobs and domestic economic benefits are more significant than contributions to the development of poorer nations? Indeed, it was reported that[25]

> Blair argued that the 280 jobs at stake on the Isle of White were more important than the government's international anti-poverty goals.

It seems that in a race between defence exports perceived as developmental tools and defence exports as contributions towards UK national prosperity and economic performance, there would only be one winner. Then the full-blooded invasion of Ukraine comes along to re-invent the narrative from defence exports as ingredients of national development to defence materials received from the United Kingdom as a critical component for national survival. In a fight to the death, the moral compass points in multiple, contradictory directions.

Notes

1 Foreign, Commonwealth and Development Office (FCDO), *The UK Government's Strategy for International Development, May 2022* (London: The Stationery Office, 2022) p. 16.
2 Michael T. Klare and Andrew T.H. Tan, 'Emerging Technologies and the Arms Trade,' in Andrew T.H Tan (Ed), *Research Handbook on the Arms Trade* (Cheltenham: Edward Elgar Publishing, 2020) p. 379.
3 Ron Matthews and Jonata Anicetti, 'Offset in a Post-Brexit World,' in *The RUSI Journal,* No. 5, 2021, p. 52.
4 Ibid.
5 Jacques S. Gansler, Democracy's Arsenal: Creating a Twenty-First-Century Defense Industry (Cambridge, MA: The MIT Press, 2011), pp. 309–318.
6 NAO 2012

7 Jon Yeomans, 'The Future of Jet Fighters Is all in the Pilot's Head,' *The Sunday Times*, July 17, 2022.
8 George Allison, 'BAE Systems Sign Type 26 contract with Australia,' in *UK Defence Journal*, 1 September 2016, https://ukdefencejournal.org.uk/bae-systems-sign-type-26-contract-australia/ accessed 9 December 2016.
9 Adrian Spragg, defence partner with Accenture, talking with the author on 13 April 2020.
10 John Louth and Trevor Taylor, *British Defence in the 21st Century* (Abingdon, OXON: Routledge, 2019) pp. 102–121.
11 Hamid E. Ali, 'Natural Resource Rents and Military Expenditure in the Middle East and North Africa: A Long-run Perspective,' in Andrew T.H. Tan (Ed) *Research Handbook on the Arms Trade* (Cheltenham: Edward Elgar Publishing, 2020) pp. 115–116
12 Ibid., p. 116. Ali provides references for a number of African and Middle Eastern empirical studies demonstrating the development effect of defence expenditure and imports. See, for example, J. Yildirin, S. Sezgin and N. Ocal, 'Military Expenditure and Economic Growth in Middle Eastern Countries: A Panel Data Analysis,' in *Defence and Peace Economics*, 2005, Vol 16, No. 4, pp. 283–295.
13 Andrew Feinstein, *The Shadow World: Inside the Global Arms Trade* (London: Hamish Hamilton, 2011) p. 188.
14 BBC Radio 4, The Today Programme, 1 October 2009, 'BAE: The Tanzanian Connection,' http://news.bbc.co.uk/today/hi/today/newsid_8284000/8284510.stm.
15 Feinstein, p. 189.
16 See the *Daily Mail,* 21 April 2008, 'BAE in New Corruption Probe as Tanzanian Minister Resigns,' http://www.dailymail.co.uk/news/article-561000/bae-new-corruption-probe-Tanzanian-minister-resigns-500-000-bribery-claim.html.
17 Feinstein, p. 193.
18 Sam Perlo-Freeman, 'Corruption in the arms trade,' in Tan (Ed), p. 100.
19 Ibid., p. 97 and p. 100.
20 UK Government, *Russian Invasion of Ukraine: UK Government Response,* https://www.gov.uk/government/topical-events/Russian-invasion-of-ukraine-uk-government-response accessed on 11th August 2022.
21 Michael Clarke, *The Challenge of Defending Britain* (Manchester: Manchester University Press, 2019).
22 Ibid, p. 100.
23 Feinstein, p. 189.
24 FCDO, 2022.
25 Feinstein, p. 190.

7 Defence Exports and National Resilience

Introduction

The notion of national resilience, and recovery post-shock, is now woven through the fabric of UK political decision-making. In regards to British defence exports as a function of that resilience, the argument presents a hypothesis that a robust and healthy defence sector helps the nation to manage in times of stress, and contributes towards the recovery from extreme strategic moments, such as the Covid-19 pandemic. The contribution to a robust, on-shore defence sector from the revenues associated with the export of arms and military services underpins, in part, this sectorial health. A solid pipeline of future orders, continual inflows of monies from sales, the potential for future export wins and the maintenance of skills and competencies in the United Kingdom to satisfy these orders, supposedly all contribute to national resilience.

This premise, though, sits on more than just the promise of revenues from overseas' sales. It is concerned with the scale of the sector, and whether it is in growth or decline. Resilience requires an ability to veer and haul between activities at times of crisis, at government direction, and to meet emerging challenges and strategic shocks through the utilization of the skills and competencies embedded throughout the sector. The argument, therefore, posits people within the defence industrial base, secured in their roles through the partial contribution of exports, as critical national resources at times of strife.

This chapter continues in the following manner. At the outset, the notion of national resilience is considered and critiqued. Thereafter, we consider the contribution of the commercial, on-shore defence sector to the dual concepts of resilience and recovery, before progressing to consider the skills and competencies contained within the sector. Finally, the possibility is offered that, following this review, a re-configured sense of resilience through defence exports might be considered by British decision-makers as a key component of modern deterrence in the United Kingdom.

DOI: 10.4324/9781003221494-7

National Resilience

The British vision of national resilience for 2030 is to possess a strengthened ability to assess, understand and manage the risks that the country could face.[1] This was made especially pertinent by the onslaught of the Covid-19 pandemic that caused chaos across health systems, economies and broadly throughout societies right across the world. In the United Kingdom alone, 200,000 people died, attributed to the pandemic, and Britain's economy contracted by almost ten percent in 2020. As a consequence, the British government argued that strategic shocks such as Covid-19:[2]

> ... demonstrated the importance of a resilient society with well developed plans and capabilities, along with flexible response structures that can adapt and respond to the unexpected.

This seems clearly sensible, but the needs for definition, context and scope of the activities associated with the state of 'resilience' seem equally important. How should society define resilience and just what are the capabilities and response structures referred to by the government?

Defining Resilience

The IR stated that government's focus, going forward, would be to build a resilient society as a strategic imperative. But the British government's own working definition of resilience can seem a little undercooked:[3]

> Traditionally, the term 'resilience' refers to an ability to withstand and quickly recover from a difficult situation. This comes hand-in hand with the idea of 'bouncing back,' of returning to 'normal,' of picking up where we left off before whatever difficulty or challenge we experienced.

Is a difficult situation the running out of bread in the morning in order to make toast or the break-up of a promising relationship? This is hardly the stuff of grand strategy and societal policy intent. Rather, resilience, as a meaningful concept beyond this flaccid and fey governmental definition, has its roots in the practices of risk management and the literature on agile institutions and behaviours. This is where it connects to the defence industrial community, sustained by exports, as will be demonstrated next.

Risk Management

In the 21st century, in certain academic circles, the act of war has increasingly been framed as a risk management strategy and preparing for war through trade a practice of risk mitigation.[4] Defence through economic transactions occurs, supposedly, to effectively manage identified risks in a functional, calculative manner. This body of research suggests that risk management, in this manner, is a function of, and positively enables, national resilience to unidentified shocks and strategic issues.

A substantial British defence industrial base, through this argument, is a purposeful and desirable component of resilience. In the early years of this century, around £34 billion was spent on defence per annum, with £6.7 billion capital equipment and infrastructure, £4.3 billion on equipment support to the military and consumables, and £2.4 billion on research and development.[5] Beyond this public spend, the commercial outputs of defence and security companies equated to just over one percent of UK economic activity.[6] National resilience, through a defence budget of two per cent of gross domestic production, sits on this commercial activity, itself enabled through defence exports – as drivers of prosperity and artefacts of national risk management.

Risk has been defined by the MoD as:[7]

> The combination of the probability of an event occurring and its consequences on objectives.

This sense of military and defence industrial responsiveness to 'risks' in the generation of national resilience is nothing new. Ahead of First World War, the development of the Dreadnought class of battleship was the subject of an argument conducted in public between the Royal Navy, politicians and industrialists around the management of the risks Britain faced from Germany and the need for maritime resilience. If Britain failed to develop these large, capital maritime weapons, the country's prestige would suffer and the country would be exposed to greater, unanswerable, firepower from continental states. A similar debate was conducted in the British press in 2007 with a discussion on the future replacement of the Trident nuclear deterrent fleet of submarines.[8]

Whilst addressing and managing risk has been a defence concern for a century or more, the National Audit Office characterizes this activity as being split distinctly between 'operational risk' and 'financial risk'.[9] The former is concerned with military outcomes, whilst the latter is associated with the costs of projects and their ongoing affordability. With the latter, the possibility of exports can be said to mitigate the costs of development, thereby contributing to UK resilience as a central theme of the defence sector.

However, effective risk management remains an informed trade-off between these two elements which can be illustrated in the case of the Apache helicopter. The British Army procured Apache for the attack-helicopter role and was deployed in Libya in 2011 and in Afghanistan until the evacuation of Western forces in 2021. The normal price of an Apache helicopter purchased from the US was £12 million – identified from the Israeli purchase of 24 aircraft in 1999.[10] For the British purchase, however, a major concern was identified through the procurement practice of attempting to manage operational risk. This was perceived as residing in US factory lines given that the lead times for components might prevent re-orders and minimize the availability of spares. For the British Government, the solution was for Westland Helicopters, a UK firm, to manage this risk on behalf of the MoD. An engineering line was established at Westland's UK headquarters to produce 67 Apache helicopters under licence from the US for the British Army. Managing the operational risk this way, unsurprisingly, increased costs. The overall cost of the programme was to be in the region of £2.5 billion, or approximately £40 million per helicopter – more than three times what Israel paid for essentially the same capability.[11]

This entanglement of themes of risk, resilience and the management practices they initiate can generate perverse effects, as in the Apache example. In terms of exports, UK development programmes assume that overseas' sales of capabilities sought by the British will reduce the costs of such programmes accrued to the UK military. In other words, exports will subsidize the unit costs of aircraft, ships or tanks bought by the British for its military: in the past, national security and resilience part-financed by Saudi Arabia's purchase of Tornado and Typhoon aircraft, for example. Suppose, for a moment, though, that this calculation of subsidy will prove to be wrong in the years ahead. Instead, assume that the unit price of Tempest will be so expensive that the UK's defence customers do not import this capability but rather depend on their existing systems. A wrong assumption around successful defence exports that, in the past, when proved correct, has contributed to prosperity and its twin, resilience, will instead, through its failure, add to a sense of national fragility and notions of defence unaffordability. Managing such a risk might require officials and industrialists to interdict in activities that, supposedly, contribute to national resilience such as research and development programmes. In this regard, the managerial logic of risk–resilience–prosperity–security might disappear in its own black hole of irrationality: the unimagined becoming the unmanageable.

Conceptual Resilience and Defence Exports

This seems significant given the strategic status offered to the notion of national resilience and those factors, such as defence exports, that can be perceived as fundamental components of such a condition. For, in the United Kingdom and more broadly across the Western security apparatus, questions of resilience have attempted to be addressed through the development and debate of concepts. An example would be, perhaps, the concept of 'deterrence by resilience' whereby Russia, for instance, might be deterred from destabilizing or even attacking NATO countries on the eastern flank of the alliance by the levels of resilience attributed to those countries.[12]

Such concepts are prevalent amongst and promoted by an eclectic community of academics, think tank practitioners and policymakers.

The contribution of revenues returned from defence exports to this notion of national resilience becomes, therefore, just a common sense, established proposition and aligns to this concept of deterrence through resilience. Such thoughts inevitably become part of the taxonomy, tools and techniques used potentially by UK defence policymakers and their influencers. However, a critique offered by some thinkers suggests that the resilience of the concepts generated themselves may be open to question:[13]

> Namely, the resilience of Western-produced (and perhaps even particularly Anglophone) strategic thought, concepts and theories … may not be, on the whole, particularly resilient, which may in fact be damaging for the West's aggregate ability to think and ultimately perform strategically.

In this regard, such a critique appears to assert that resilience might be a fashionable trend in defence thinking with all manner of contributions (such as defence exports) driving its stance and status. But, in fact, resilience is an imposter at the ball of strategic thinking where the moves of the dance are timeless and enduring. These are centred on a foundation understanding of strategy, war, conflict and security derived from thinkers and practitioners such as von Clausewitz.[14] Resilience might be superficially attractive but, over time, comes to lack substance in the company of the founding knowledge of grand strategy.

Such a critique assumes that grand strategy itself possesses a special status of truth and deep understanding. This is the stuff of theology rather than a clear-eyed analysis that goes to the heart of the subject of strategic studies. This discipline and its core theory of strategy generate a tangentially different understanding of theory than other, related, realms of study such as political science of economics. The body of knowledge associated with social sciences more broadly seeks to model and explain causal relationships based on observation and modelling with an intent towards predictive outcomes. Raising interest rates, for example, is intended to cool the economy thereby countering the rise in inflation. Such an outcome is predictable based on knowledge of previous economic events. Such observations, in turn, through application become an economic norm or 'rule.' In contrast, strategic theory is a whole-system body of knowledge relating to war and strategy which excludes other explanations or insights. It represents, in effect, a single comprehensive theory based on the writings of Carl von Clausewitz.[15]

Defence exports from the United Kingdom, though, undoubtedly are concerned with materials of war and contribute towards a robust, on-shore defence sector. Such things are inevitably strategic in nature and concerned with deterring wars of fighting them as effectively and efficiently as possible. Rejecting the significance of notions of resilience to these spaces and places on 'true believer,' strategic studies as theology grounds, seems flawed. It is counter-instructive to those in boardrooms and ministries charged with generating defence, security and industrial policies in and for the real world.

A Word on Agility

In seeking a more pragmatic view of grans theory and resilience, we could also note that the literature on agile organizations suggests that resilient societies have a readiness to tolerate failure but are committed to learning from experience. They possess, also, core competencies on mass within specific sectors of the economy.[16] The logic offered is that a sense of agility is needed to survive and respond to crises, and thus societies and their businesses seeking a resilient posture must develop their risk management, crisis management and business continuity capabilities. In the United Kingdom, this sense of responsiveness and agility is a feature of modern business practices within the defence sector. One area of research especially significant to our analysis is the twin-importance of a robust and flexible supply chain and the near-certainty of a pipeline of future orders and revenues – hence the attractiveness of defence exports.

A substantial literature on business resilience and business continuity – as agility – has developed this century, much of which emphasizes the importance of the duplication of assets, integration of technologies and the management of working capital. The key feature, however, has become the competencies within a sector and a focus on behaviours as a key tool in response to crises. From this academic body of knowledge, resilience, as the capacity to adapt in order to survive shocks, has become a focus of attention and significant to those who champion defence exports from the United Kingdom.[17]

Resilience, Competencies, and Defence Sales

Revenues, Defence People, and Resilience

When it comes to notions of resilience, therefore, the relationship between the British Government and the defence and security businesses that operate within its borders is complicated and, as we have seen, witnessed through multiple understandings and preferences. At one extreme, is the concept of the defence-industrial complex: a powerful, politically in-tune commercial sector feeding constantly on government money and permissions for sales overseas. In contrast, others may see defence industry in the United Kingdom as an important capability partner to the British military, directly supporting operations on the frontline and contributing to British military collaboration with other powers.

Other understandings may favour notions of the UK defence industrial base as a British national hub of knowledge, equipment and support, able to respond to challenges and surge outputs to meet national targets at a moment of crisis. British government revenues and sales to friendly countries, in this regard, nourish a strategic national reserve of skills and capacity that is critical for resilience and recovery:[18]

> Common to these latter perspective, perhaps, is the sense that the skills and competencies of the defence-industrial worker are important to standing ideas around national security and international obligations; that critical skills relating to defence capability actually reside with the folk in overalls on the factory floor as well as with those in military uniforms.

In part, these skills, necessary for this sense of national resilience, are the hard-edged engineering and project management skills found in the sector. The largest defence business headquartered in the United Kingdom, BAE Systems, is the UK's largest single employer of engineers and engineering project management staff – substantial applicable knowledge and intellectual capital residing in the sector.

A large study of this company revealed that, at a particular moment, ten percent of the cohort under review was employed in project management. Twenty-five percent of the study population were employed as engineers and another ten percent worked as information technology specialists. These are the very skills necessary for an agile and resilient economy and society. A case can be made, therefore, for this causal link between revenues earned from defence exports and the resilience of the United Kingdom.

The data itself illuminates this point. In 2020, BAE Systems spent £93 million on the development of skills, direct training and other development goals across its workforce, and on engagement with schools and young people. In this year, also, the company supported a total contribution to the UK Exchequer of a sum equal to £2.7 billion.[19] In broad terms, this figure equates to the combined operating budgets of the Cabinet Office, the Department for International Trade and HM Treasury. At the same time, the value of goods and services exported by BAE Systems to customers around the world equalled £3.9 billion.[20] There seems a clear correlation between these sums earned through exports and the direct and indirect contributions to the country's finances. The narrative of the defence sector's largest business contributing to national revenues, national skills and, therefore, national resilience seems compelling. Indeed, as the Chairman, Sir Roger Carr, commented:[21]

> With 72 percent of our UK workforce in highly skilled engineering-related roles, we are closely aligned with the UK Government's focus on skills.

In contrast to the bulk of a BAE Systems, the British defence SME, Subsea Craft Ltd., a manufacturer of a maritime convertible prototype, is also focussed on the resilience agenda. The military challenges of the next

20–30 years will be varied and unpredictable. There will be a need to penetrate and access an adversary's geographical area of control in the period ahead, and Subsea Craft's submersible rapid raider, the VICTA, is designed to puncture an enemy's operating space. The concept and prototype are based on the calculation that the desire to regain military and political initiatives from rival states, below the threshold of armed conflict, through the traditional tools of sabotage, subterfuge, and deniable action will be attractive to those countries that benefit from UK defence exports. There is, therefore, a need for an asset that grows and builds military response options for political leaders, with covert and deniable access at speed and range. Such a platform opens a portal to new avenues of horizontal escalation, de-escalation and coercion that have previously been bounded by the platform restrictions of conventional maritime ships and large, expensive submarines.

Subsea Craft is a small business financed through private equity that is built upon the potential for defence exports as the company does not expect to sell to the Royal Navy. Rather, it sees success as a combination of sensible profits through overseas' sales and the building of resilience in the United Kingdom through the development of skills and competencies at its home city of Portsmouth. As Scott Verney, the CEO, says of the business proposition:[22]

> We do two things brilliantly. First, we offer a critical capability to the UK's allies in VICTA and benefit from the UK's support to defence exports. Second, we contribute to the country's resilience through the championing and employment of great engineers, technologists and problem solvers.

The business case for VICTA is based on the debate in government and defence circles relating to a military's future operating environment that suggests that emerging concepts of operation for the VICTA class are more fluid and contingent than those associated with more conventional and readily identified capability requirements. Namely, that the shifts in geopolitical considerations and the actions of competitor states and potential rivals allow VICTA to fill emerging capability gaps, offering risk mitigation and resilience to allies through exports from the United Kingdom.

At its most orthodox, VICTA is a surface or sub-surface maritime insertion and interdiction craft. Characteristically, it possesses an independent surface long-range insertion proposition of 240 nautical miles at a speed of up to 30 knots. On arrival at a surface-to-sub-surface transition point, VICTA can convert to a mini-submarine, hiding below the waves, within two minutes. The craft is configured optimally to cruise sub-surface at six knots for a range of 25 nautical miles. Therefore, the orthodox use of VICTA is the clandestine insertion and recovery of special forces or maritime operators into a target area, utilizing personal breathing apparatus. In this regard, the command module has the capacity for one pilot and one co-pilot, both of whom can operate the craft independently, whilst the payload compartment houses up to six special forces operators.

At a price point yet to be decided, but significantly cheaper than the cost of a conventional frigate or submarine, Subsea Craft believes that it can enter the defence exports market, provide exquisite technologies to the UK's allies whilst, concurrently building capacity and maximizing skills at home. Both the large international conglomerate of a group such as BAE Systems and a small, niche technology business, such as Subsea Craft, can be homed in this debate on resilience: a narrative that can be sensibly located right through the defence sector in the UK.

Across the savanna of UK defence and industrial policy making, there does not yet seem to be an overt link between the revenues earned by businesses through defence exports, the skills these earning support, the tax revenues paid to the UK Exchequer, the agility offered to allies and the United Kingdom, national notions of resilience. This seems odd, given the national narrative on resilience and the central role that appears to be played by defence companies big and small. It is speculative at the time of writing, but this seems rich ground for advocates of defence industries to plough in the years ahead. Already, one can sense public relations companies reaching for their calculators.

Resilience and Deterrence in the Grey Zone

The sense of national robustness acquired and maintained through the skills, competencies, industrial mass and revenues generated through overseas' defence sales points to, as hinted above, a critical deterrence function associated fundamentally with the concept of resilience. Whilst Russia's invasion of Ukraine represents a disturbing 'hot' war, altering the strategic calculations of states in Europe and beyond, 'grey zone' aggression has taken place in the notional zone between a state of kinetic warfare and cooperative peace. Such grey zone activities, short of war, are used by aggressor nations to weaken and destabilize a target country. China's punitive tariffs on Australian wine imports, from 2020, could be perceived as a grey zone operation as indeed must the Salisbury attacks on the UK from Russia in 2018.[23] In the case of Australian wine:[24]

> The Australian wine industry relies heavily on exports, shipping 60 percent of its production overseas. In less than a decade, China soared to the top of that export list, becoming Australia's first AUD $1 billion a year wine market in 2019. Until recently, China accounted for 39 percent of all Australian wine exports.

As a result of frayed and competitive geopolitical relationships between China and Australia, tariffs on Australian wine were raised to between 116 and 218 percent on bottled Australian wine imports, to be imposed until

2026, effectively destroying Australia's largest export market. By the end of 2021, a year after the first round of tariffs, were initiated, the value of Australian wine exports to China had shrunk by 97 percent, whilst global exports of Australian wine contracted by 30 percent, pre-tariff values. Grey zone aggressions, such are these, can be enormously impactful economically and socially.

Not surprisingly, China and Russia are said to be the main exponents of grey zone attacks, specifically targeting a nation's politics, civil society, industrial strategy and national infrastructure. As a consequence, notions of national deterrence in the United Kingdom are beginning to migrate from those associated with major military strategic assets, such as nuclear-armed submarines, to civil society itself, with societal and industrial resilience forming a key platform of modern deterrence.

As understandings develop relating to the concept of the resilient state and society, in an era of grey zone threats, policy proposals continue to emerge.[25] These range from strengthening citizen resilience through programmes of voluntary resilience training, in the case of the general public, through to mandatory training for key workers, however, defined. Beyond these suggestions, there have been calls for the introduction of resilience exercises to interdict and quickly recover from the effects of grey zone attacks. A bounded and identifiable community of defence private sector professionals, in part assured through the revenues of exports, is an ideal starting point for resilience-practitioner development.[26]

Conclusion

The proposition of this chapter is fairly straightforward. National resilience, as a concept, has entered the political lexicon following shocks such as the attacks on the United States in 2001, and the global pandemic commencing in 2019. The United Kingdom has defined it, paraphrased, as the ability to face up to a strategic shock, absorb it and recover quickly from its effects. Academically, the concept is derived from the literature on agility and the commercial and project practices of risk and opportunity management. For the defence sector in the UK, contributions to resilience are made through the employment and training of engineers, scientists, technologists and project management professionals. The revenues earned from overseas' sales enable the development of this national body of expertise, thereby contributing directly to the country's resilience. Moreover, the taxation paid on such sales combined with the income taxes applied to employees, represent substantial sums paid to the government, allowing it to undertake various activities. Advocates of this argument promote it as a virtuous circle of revenues to resilience, and, indeed, there does appear to be a case to be made. As demonstrated with our examples of a large, international corporation and a niche defence SME, both companies view themselves, and their potential exports, as exemplars of national resilience and responsiveness.

It is, of course, an argument based on orthodoxy rather than science: a causal link between the appeal and commerciality of defence materials generated in the United Kingdom and the country's stewardship in regard to resilience is beyond the social scientist and business student. This author believes, however, that it is an argument citizens will hear with evermore conviction, not least from executives sitting in defence companies' boardrooms.

Notes

1 The Cabinet Office, The National Resilience Strategy: A Call for Evidence (London: CO, 2021) https://assets.publishing.service.gov.uk/government/uploads.system/uploads/attachment_data/file/1001404/Resilience_Strategy_-_Call_for_Evidence.pdf
2 Ibid., p. 7.
3 Ibid., p. 12.
4 Yee-Kuang Heng, *War as Risk Management* (Abingdon: Routledge, 2006).
5 Henrik Heidenkamp, John Louth, and Trevor Taylor, *The Defence Industrial Ecosystem* (London: RUSI, 2011).
6 Malcolm Chalmers, 'The Lean Years: Defence Consequences of the Fiscal Crisis,' in Michael Codner and Michael Clarke (Eds), *A Question of Security* (London: IB Tauris, 2011).
7 Ministry of Defence, *The Smart Acquisition Handbook* (Ed. 5), (London: MoD, 2004) p. 31.
8 Bill Kincaid, *Changing the Dinosaur's Spots* (London: RUSI, 2008).
9 National Audit Office C&AG's Report (NAO), *MoD Major Projects Report* (London: The Stationery Office, 2005).
10 Lewis Page, *Lions, Donkeys and Dinosaurs* (London: William Heinemann, 2006).
11 NAO, 2005.
12 Stephen J. Flanagan, *Deterring Russian Aggression in the Baltic States Through Resilience and Resistance* (RAND Corporation, 2019).
13 Lukas Milevski, 'Conceptual Resilience Versus Social Utility in Strategic Thinking,' in *RUSI Journal,* 2022, No. 2, p. 62.
14 Chiara Libiseller and Lukas Milevski, 'War and Peace: Reaffirming the Distinction,' in *Survival,* 2021, Vol 63, No. 1, pp. 101-112.
15 Carl von Clausewitz, *On War* (Ed and Trans. Michael Howard and Peter Paret (Princeton: Princeton University Press, 1989).
16 M.Syrett and M.Devine, 'Agility' chapter in *Managing Uncertainty: Strategies for Surviving and Thriving in Turbulent Times* (London: The Economist, 2012) pp.84–6; McKinsey & Company, 'Disruptive Entrepreneurs: an interview with Eric Ries' April 2014.
17 C. Lehane, M.Fabiani & B. Guttenberg, *Masters of Disaster: the Ten Commandments of Damage Control* (London: Palgrave MacMillan, 2012).
18 John Louth, Trevor Taylor and Henrik Heidenkamp, *RUSI Briefing Paper: Defence Skills, A Shift in the Myth* (London: RUSI, 2014) p. 2.
19 Oxford Economics, *BAE Systems Contribution to the UK Economy* (Oxford: OE, 2022). https://www.baesystems.com/en-media/uploadFile/20211221140800/1573670986028.pdf
20 Ibid.
21 Ibid., p. 2.
22 Interview with Scott Verney of Subsea Craft, 30 July 2022.

23 Russian intelligence agents are alleged to have attacked a dissident target with Novichok in the British city of Salisbury in March 2018.

24 https://www.winemag.com/2022/03/10/china-australia-wine-tariffs/

25 See, for example, the work of Elisabeth Braw, *The Defender's Dilemma: Defining, Identifying and Deterring Grey Zone Aggression* (Washington, DC: American Enterprise Institute, 2021).

26 Ibid.

8 Technologies, Transfers, and Defence Exports

Introduction

At the end of the Second World War, the United Kingdom was exhausted and broke, facing a period of economic retrenchment and social transformation as the British Empire was to morph into the Commonwealth over the next decades.[1] There was to be a social revolution in the 70 years or so from 1945 that would witness the concept of the nuclear family being revolutionized, responses to questions of gender reshaped from 1950s' understandings, and the country altered for the better through immigration, principally from the old empire. One constant from this period of exponential change was the UK's national security strategy, which was based on technological superiority. This followed the policy stance of successive US governments which were determined to offset the Soviet Union and Warsaw Pact's quantitative military superiority by investing in, and rolling-out to fighting forces, exquisite technologies. A cornerstone of the UK's defence posture today is a recognition that British industry, part-financed by government:[2]

> … must develop advanced technology, anticipate how advanced technology (military and commercial) will be used in the future and who will use it, and develop technological and or operational counters to each of these.

Research and development, therefore, is crucial to this effort but investing in new technologies for defence businesses is usually an expensive proposition. There needs to be a sense of the anticipated returns on those investments before decisions to proceed with research can be made in boardrooms. The UK's national security strategy, therefore, in part, has been outsourced to the preferences of company's investment committees.

This is significant for defence exports in a number of ways. The volumes of units produced by a technology-rich defence asset can offset the scale of the initial investment. The more units sold, the greater the contribution towards the cost of research and development. Overseas markets, therefore, either through collaborative, international programmes or direct exports,

DOI: 10.4324/9781003221494-8

become hugely significant to this calculation. Second, the drumbeat and regularity of returns through overseas' sales enable companies to reinvest in new research and development – and so the cycle continues. Thus, BAE Systems was able to invest £1.1 billion in research and development in 2020.[3]

This chapter considers the concept of defence exports through the multiple facets of technological development and utility within defence systems. It considers the challenges – and opportunities – of the management of proprietary materials, ideas and assets, and the twin dynamics of intellectual property and national secrecy. The chapter notes, also, that some companies in the UK defence arena are beginning to focus on overseas markets ahead of sales to the British armed forces and wonder how this trend will develop. Finally, there is a section considering the specific challenges of Tempest, the future combat aircraft, as an exemplar, and considers how these could be addressed by governmental, commercial and military stakeholders.

The Importance of Technology

In the very particular taxonomy of defence in the United Kingdom, government officials, industrialists, politicians and military commanders use words such as 'research,' 'development,' 'science,' and 'technology' continually and, often, interchangeably. There are, though, clear definitions that should be applied. Governments and businesses that spend on research into new technologies, or in the search for new applications for existing technologies, are indulging in the following:

- Pure research – activities to advance knowledge through science and technology enquiry;
- Applied research – the exploitation of pure research towards a specified objective or outcome; and
- Development – activities linked to a known and identified programme or project.

The distinctions are important in business as there are different accounting treatments relating to each activity under these definitions. Typically, pure research is general business expenditure and is an annual cost of doing business, whilst applied research and development contributes to work in progress and is captured on a company's balance sheet as an asset. For the former, a business can recover the VAT paid against pure research, which is not the case for programmed and targeted applied research and development. For niche, technology businesses, the VAT refund in the early years is a major contributor to working capital. Definitions, therefore, matter very much for businesses trading-off cash flows against revenues from orders, as the company grows and begins to trade.

Across the defence enterprise in the United Kingdom, science and technology expenditure is associated with this notion of pure research. Within the defence budget, historically, this has been targeted at 1.2 percent of the total defence spent, or about £0.5 billion. Applied research and development spending can be found across the Equipment Plan of the MoD, and represent monies already committed to certain programmes and projects generating defence capabilities.

It can be seen from this summary that, given the relatively modest amount of money associated with pure research provided from the government over the past few decades, companies operating in this sector have had to commit their own resources into research exploring new or evolving defence items. Not unreasonably, these businesses and shareholders require reasonable returns. This poses all manner of issues as we shall come on to discover.

Also, the rapid development of science and technology applicability poses challenges to the country as a whole that are hard to interdict or deter through the efforts of the British military. The rules-based order of the international system is being eroded by political disruption and ever-faster technologically driven change. The protection of critical national infrastructure is now a very real defence issue: power stations, hospitals, transport hubs and banks, for example, can all be endangered by cyber-attacks. Unfriendly states and groups no longer need a strategic air force or armoury of intercontinental ballistic missiles to threaten the physicality of the British homeland and peoples: a networked computer terminal with a little know-how will suffice. Therefore, applied research and development activities need to be spread wider than ever, and shifted beyond merely focusing on traditional defence assets such as aircraft and ships.[4]

> The manner in which the UK flexibly adopts and adapts technologies in this search for security has become a defence imperative. We can only begin to imagine the ways in which biomedicine, artificial intelligence, robotics, the internet and quantum computing will transform the UK and its place in the world. Our ability to be safe and prosperous, in part at least, is dependent upon how we can protect, secure and assure these strategic modern utilities.

If this is reasonable, research and development into technological transformation will become increasingly focussed on homeland security. The scope for revenues from overseas' sales associated with conventional defence exports might diminish. Moreover, permissions for export from the UK government might wain in the case of technologies critical to our own core security. Research is hugely important to exports in the defence market, but it also drives government intervention to keep secret what is critical to the United Kingdom.

Intellectual Property, Ownership, and Security

So far, this book has suggested that, throughout this century, UK defence exports have been dominated by the aerospace sector. The significant exception, of course, has been the export victory of BAE Systems in providing the Type 26 frigate design to Australia. The UK's submarine fleet is entirely nuclear-based with, traditionally, no opportunities for exports: military nuclear-propulsion solutions are protected onshore as a matter of government policy. That stance might shift under AUKUS arrangements as the British consider making nuclear submarine technologies available to the Australians.

In terms of systems for the land domain in the United Kingdom, and the subsequent potential for exports, Britain has allowed the land vehicle industry to shrink with the closure of tank plants in Newcastle and Leeds. The British Army was compelled to generate its core land vehicle system, Ajax, from general Dynamics, an American-headquartered defence conglomerate though, in fairness, assembly and elements of manufacture were to be undertaken in the United Kingdom by the business.[5] Major British defence exports, consequently, are, not surprisingly, typically related to aircraft and, belatedly, ships. The exception, perhaps, is smart munitions from companies such as MBDA.

This is important because aircraft and ships are rich in technology and British integration ingenuity which both the government and businesses want to protect from falling into the hands of those who would threaten the United Kingdom. For the companies in question, that technology is often the result of blended investment from themselves and early research project monies from the British Government. There is, from this investment, a value on the company's balance sheet relating to these technologies that is a major asset to the business. This is owned by shareholders who demand sound husbandry and proper returns on their investment: consequently, the interests of shareholders and governments might not always align. Exquisite technologies, though, integrated onto defence platforms, cannot be spread around or exported at a whim. Rather, there are clear protections in place, directed by the government, to which companies must offer legal compliance.

For a business to export secret technologies or systems to a third-party nation,[6] the MoD has to give approval via an administrative process involving information gathered on a document called Form 680. This is in addition to the export licences necessary from the Department for International Trade. The technologies owned by the company are clearly regulated by the state, placing a restriction on how a company can exploit its assets. Also[7]

> The Form 680 and the export licence processes are clearly related but technically separate. The MoD may approve the release of information to a prospective customer only for the government to later decide that it should not allow the actual export of the product.

Overseas state clients, however, are attracted to the potential export in the first place by the very technologies that the British seek to protect. Given this, for that technology to be released, there needs to be an alignment of interests between the UK government, the receiving government and the supplying business. A good example of this is the Type 26-Hunter frigate programme.

The Type 26 frigate was chosen as the design basis for the Australian Hunter Class programme. This was, for the Australians, principally about the transfer of maritime technologies and know-how, from the United Kingdom, to recapitalize Australian maritime industrial capacity. For the deal to go ahead, it was important to the Federal and the South Australian state governments for construction to be at the Osborne shipbuilding facility near Adelaide in South Australia, by an Australian workforce, employed by BAE Systems.[8]

This is significant. The erstwhile Australian Defence Minister, Christopher Pyne, informed the author that the Hunter programme encapsulated the very essence of Australian defence policy ambition, anchored in UK technology.[9] First, the capability for force projection and manoeuvre offers the Australian Defence Force a deterrence and defeat maritime capability focussed predominantly on its near neighbours and northern waters. Beyond that, going forward, by developing this national capability *in tandem* with the United Kingdom through BAE Systems, the rigour of an industrial collaborative programme contributes overtly to core Australian defence values of innovation, teamwork and the importing of technical solutions new to the Australian force structure. Based on the UK knowledge base, programmes such as Hunter become, somehow, quintessentially Australian and 'local' – 'the way we do defence in my country'[10] – whilst also being international and dependent on another nation's defence industrial base.

This initial technological insertion into the Australian defence ecosystem is important and points to the significance of technology in strategic exports from the United Kingdom. Somehow, though, geography still matters and the Australian defence policy-making community continue to face challenges around the development of strategic partnership with countries, such as Indonesia, in their near-home waters. Whilst struggling with these immediate geopolitical challenges, Australian commanders also need to integrate new technologies (secured from the United Kingdom) with and across older platforms, legacy systems and develop refreshed military doctrine. In this regard, the importation of new technologies allows the Australians to develop from fresh the capabilities, competencies and capacities necessary for a uniformed-civilian defence stance, combining the best efforts of the industrialist and war-fighter.[11]

But what about the British? Using an emerging collaborative programme such as the Type 26-Hunter class, post a competition, and the associated technology transfers, to build defence industrial capability in Australia might cause concern in the United Kingdom that its actions could have destroyed a valuable export market, long-term dependent on UK products. Indeed, British policymakers might even have created a future competitor for the next generation of defence exports. However, whilst Australia is gaining design as well as construction capabilities under the Hunter class programme, much of the transfer is moving from one part of the same, UK-headquartered, company, BAE Systems, to another in a foreign jurisdiction, controlled by UK defence exports' rules. Moreover, looking forward, the United Kingdom can expect to find large national projects to be unaffordable and will need collaborating countries to join with the United Kingdom in providing finance. Of course, this is currently the case with the Tempest programme which is considered later in this chapter. Thus, the Hunter class can be seen less as the UK building up a potential competitor, and more as strengthening a desired collaborative partnership through deliberate, strategically assessed technology transfers.

Intellectual Property

Central to this debate on technology transfers and the significance of research and development is the notion of intellectual property (IP). This is a form of property that has been created by human thought and ingenuity, in commerce, tested often through scientific enquiry. In the defence sector, it is usually associated with specific brands or identifiable new technologies, post-research. In the case of a brand, its value as an intangible asset is identified, often, post-acquisition by a third party. The value of a specific technology can prove to be more challenging prior to product sales.

Intellectual property laws allow businesses to possess property rights to the information and intellectual goods they have generated. In the case of the defence market, a significant component of the price of a major asset, such as an aircraft, is represented by the IP of the technologies being integrated. The challenge, of course, is that technology as an intellectual concept – knowledge, if you like – is indivisible and an infinite number of people can learn it, consume it and, eventually, amend and improve upon it. Technology, therefore, can be copied, so, once it is beyond the physical control of owners, rival states can plunder IP for the development of their own systems.

This has to be considered by boardrooms when deciding upon overseas' sales. Whilst the UK government will wish to protect IP developed in the United Kingdom for defence purposes and possess an export approval system so to do, company directors have to weigh the exposure of their specific IP against potential revenues earned. In this regard, the interests of the government are not always aligned to the business decisions of a board of directors. The UK government might be keen to bolster a bilateral agreement with another state through defence sales, only for the company to deduce that home market sales and protected IP trump overseas revenues. Conversely, the company might be content with exposing its IP to a third-party state, only for the government to decline approvals, intent on keeping that knowledge onshore.[12]

The obvious point, though, is that, whilst the company might own the technology in question and have protected intellectual property rights, it does not possess exclusive *control* over its asset. Rather, it is an asset of interest to both business and government with both having a deciding role of how, or even, if, it is to be exported off-shore. This can be a shock to investors and executives new to defence.

Exports Without Home Sales

The successful integration of new or reworked technologies into defence assets has been at the heart of the UK's order of battle for generations. The sense is that the successful utility of the product with the British military drives exports as friendly nations seek to import the capability witnessed in use with the Royal Air Force, for example. This is certainly a correct assumption in the case of Hawk and Typhoon sales to the Middle East.

This suggests that exports occur where technologies and products from UK companies are usually employed first by the British Military. Indeed, the export control regime seems to have this as a basic operating assumption whereby materials classified by the British Government, deployed on British military assets, are assessed for suitability of transfer to allies. Some companies based in the United Kingdom, though, have, as their strategic plan, the core concept of defence exports to third parties without any sales to the British. This is a fairly new phenomenon.

Subsea Craft Ltd is such an example, a defence SME which seeks to sell a small, maritime craft to overseas militaries without the asset's first use with the Royal Navy. This poses a number of challenges. First, potential client nations can reasonably ask why the British have no use for the craft, which could impinge upon direct sales. Second, private equity and other potential defence investors might prove less keen on investing without British military endorsement. Third, the technology that comprises the craft will be exposed to, and utilized by, allied nations ahead of the United Kingdom. As the technology within the craft has not been classified by the British government and is not subject to MoD approval via the Form 680 process, early adopter nations might find additional uses for the technologies in question, or themselves, seek to develop and enhance the craft within their own borders for future exports. At an extreme, the British military might, long term, be challenged by research and development generated in the United Kingdom by a British business. That would not be the intention, of course, but control of technology is a challenge once it leaves British shores. Such scenarios, of UK defence businesses not having a home market, are increasing. It will prove necessary for both the security regime and export approvals process to change in order to take account of this reality.

Technological Collaboration and Exports: Tempest

Since the First World War, the United Kingdom has always developed and deployed combat air systems.[13] Today, the RAF's principal combat air systems are the Typhoon and F35b Lightning II aircraft.[14] The Strategic

Defence and Security Review of 2015, and the Modernizing Defence Programme that followed a little later in 2018, asserted the importance of air power as a dominant strategic force. The capability was said to possess an unrivalled ability for speed, depth of penetration and flexibility in interdicting multiple threats.[15] The Future Combat Air Strategy[16] also acknowledged that the Typhoon and F35b force mix would be the backbone of UK combat air until the mid-2030s, with Typhoon gradually phased from service between now and then. Consequently, the UK's future combat air system, Tempest, is set to fill the capability gap left by Typhoon. In the early years of service, it will also complement the UK fleet of F35b aircraft that fly from British aircraft carriers. Importantly, tempest will enable a significant uplift of military capability associated with sixth-generation combat aircraft design, support and operation.

This ambition is built on the rapid research, development, test and evaluation of exquisite and disruptive technologies, developed in the United Kingdom and across partner nations, generating a range of air capabilities that are truly revolutionary. These technologies are to be sourced from partners, in part, working collaboratively, and exported to partners also, in a complex, and expensive, international joint venture involving the governments of Britain, Italy, Sweden, and Japan. In the United Kingdom, BAE Systems, Rolls-Royce, Leonardo, and MBDA are at the heart of the commercial solution.

The concept is for the home-nations of the programme to purchase and use Tempest as their air combat solution from the mid-30s, as well as undertaking a strategic programme of business development and marketing leading to significant exports to other allies. Once more, the twin-tracks of revenues and technologies underscore a defence sector proposition.

But the need is clear and obvious. The weight of evidence in the public domain supports the view that Russia and China have developed the surveillance and precision strike capabilities to put at serious risk Western military assets including today's aircraft and future air systems.[17] Indeed, the ranges of Russia's anti-ship and anti-air missiles are extending as are their potency.[18] The Russians have been focused on developing ground-based anti-air defences for a long time, and the sensors and missiles ranges involved are now able to reach the areas and heights where Western aircraft operate. Tempest, therefore, has to be developed to operate in a non-permissive environment where its survivability is anything but assured.

The technologies associated with Tempest represent a cornerstone of the UK's industrial strategy as, onshore:[19]

> Defence's contribution to GDP includes over £7bn of exports generated on average each year in addition to the MoD budget of £37bn. [The MoD's] role as a customer and industrial partner with high growth sectors in the economy generates more growth … [and] is very valuable, both to the ability of the Armed Forces to deploy successfully and to keep the UK ahead of its competitors and adversaries in the future.

In addition, the UK combat air sector has a turnover in excess of £6 billion per annum and has contributed over four-fifths of defence exports from the United Kingdom in the past decade.[20] Put simply, partner nations have bought aircraft and air systems from the United Kingdom and the government and partners of Tempest believe that this will continue. It is, of course, a main programme assumption that will be tested in the market by the future price per unit associated with the aircraft. For near-peer allies, it might be simply unaffordable come the mid-1930s, which could undermine the programme's cost model and notions of affordability for the partner nations as well.

Possessing an onshore, technology-rich forward programme for Tempest, focused on partner nations and exports to third parties, is critical in allowing the United Kingdom to maintain and enhance a proven, innovative industrial base. Within this, properly funded, disruptive research and development can flourish, reshaping the technological map for air power. This could not happen without the strategic prize of exports, recovering – and offering a return – on significant governmental and commercial technological investment. Choices around the delivery of future requirements – at home and abroad – paradoxically allow for the continued operation, maintenance and upgrade of the United Kingdom's current fleet of aircraft as well: it is one and the same workforce, after all.

Whilst the United Kingdom has been successful in the past at generating military aircraft exports, designing capability for the national need and for exports over a long planning horizon can be extremely difficult, given the complexities of requirements and uncertainties around future operating environments. This is before tricky issues such as affordability and the defence budgets of allies are considered. However, the MoD is mindful that a number of current combat aircraft types meet notional out-of-service dates in the mid-to-late 2030s. Having available a proven air system, Tempest, in the early years of its service with the RAF, fully integrated with the F35b and other defence systems, represents a once-in-a-generation opportunity for exports and influence.[21]

> Fourth generation combat aircraft … Typhoon, Rafale, F-16, F-18 and Gripen, will start to be retired from service in the late 2030s … there will be a significant market for a successor to these capabilities over the period 2040–2060. The UK's experience in developing Tornado and Typhoon, on the F-35 programme and integrating 4th and 5th generation systems means we are ideally placed to work with a wide range of partners to achieve first mover advantage within this market.

That this opportunity for exports and influence is, at heart, a technological research, development and integration endeavour is the key point. Without such critical technology, in this instance homed in Tempest, there could be no exports. Yet, without the cash flows promised from exports, there could be no programme plan to execute Tempest as a national defence asset. This interdependency, in many ways, is the core understanding of defence exports, as we move to the middle years of this century.

Conclusion

UK defence exports are, at their core, the transfer of technologies essential for military utility from the United Kingdom to an overseas partner. The technology itself is protected by IP law, UK security classifications and an export licencing regime. The governmental controls are challenged when the defence business does not possess, or seek to have, a home market and exists solely for exports. In such a case, neither the product nor the technologies it contains are classified by the UK government and overseas powers receive their benefits instead of the home nation. The British military remains in ignorance of the capabilities concerned and British officials unsighted on the potential of the technologies.

Where both the British government and industry understand the potency of the technologies integrated within the shell of the defence product, it is often important to view the development of such technologies, at inception, as a collaboration between friendly nations. There is, of course, the potential for future exports beyond the key partners and such a calculation forms part of the business case, as we have seen with the Tempest programme. But for the British to 'go alone,' especially in the cases of aerospace and smart weapons, it is probably unaffordable and places too much of a supply-side and capital burden on the businesses hosted in the United Kingdom. The exporting of defence technologies, therefore, enables the development of the UK's own defence capabilities and is critical to the UK's national security.

This is not appreciated by everybody. The campaigner and activist, opposed to the international trade in arms, might reject the development of technologies for lethal purposes. The business director, new to defence, might balk at the investment a business is expected by the government to make into early research and development on next-generation capabilities, given the single-digit returns on investment businesses are projected to make. Technology, though, is the life-blood of both the modern practice of defence and a key driver of British defence exports: and as its development becomes ever more rapid and complex, with the potential for transformation change, its importance to defence exports, can be expected to increase. For, there are[22]

> … major step changes in military technology on the horizon that will reshape the future character of warfare … [T]he role of high-speed platforms and systems, including hypersonics and directed energy weapons (DEW) adds a new dimension of warfare – high-speed warfare – with DEW potentially reducing the cost of projecting force to 'cents per shot' compared to traditional guided weapons.

Notes

1 Stephen J. Lee, *Aspects of European History 1789–1980* (London: Methuen and Co, 1982) pp. 293–305.

2 Jacques S. Gansler, *Democracy's Arsenal: Creating a Twenty-Firs-Century Defense Industry* (Cambridge, MA: The MIT Press, 2011) p. 253.

3 https://www.baesystems.com/en-media/uploadFile/20211221140800/1573670986028.pdf

4 John Louth and Trevor Taylor, *British Defence in the 21st Century* (Abingdon: Routledge, 2019) p. 70.

5 The Ajax programme has been mired in controversy with the House of Commons Defence Select Committee describing the system unfit-for-purpose and the acquisition programme a failure.

6 The United Kingdom has a classification system of materials, technologies and information that ran, traditionally, in ascending order from RESTRICTED to TOP SECRET. This has been modified and expanded over the years. MoD approval is required for the release of information or equipment classified OFFICIAL-SENSITIVE and above to foreign entities. This is a very low bar for approvals, covering most items that could be exported from a defence company that does business with the UK government.

7 Louth and Taylor, p. 110.

8 Gabby Costigan, CEO BAE Systems Australia, speaking at the Australian High Commission in London on 9 September 2019.

9 Speaking with the Hon. Christopher Pyne, Australian Defence Minister, 9 October 2018, Sydney, Australia.

10 Mr Tony Fraser, Deputy Secretary Australian Capability Acquisition and Sustainment Group, speaking to the author on 11 September 2019, London.

11 Peter Jennings, 'Do we need another defence white paper and what should it say?' ASPI, The *Strategist*, 26 February 2019.

12 There are issues of commercial confidentiality here as well as secrecy issues. Informants will only provide background or information off the record.

13 See Michael Fopp, *Spirit of the Royal Air Force: One Hundred Years of Excellence* (Oxford: Chris Andrews Publications, 2018).

14 Justin Bronk, *Maximum Value from the F-35: Harnessing Transformational Fifth-generation Capabilities for the UK Military* (London: RUSI Whitehall Report 1–16, February 2016).

15 HM Government, *National Security Strategy and Strategic Defence and Security Review 2015: A Secure and Prosperous United Kingdom*, Cm 9161 (London: The Stationery Office, November 2015).

16 Ministry of Defence, *Combat Air Strategy: An ambitious Vision for the Future* (London: MoD, 2018).

17 Fabrice Pothier, 'An Area-Access Strategy for NATO', *Survival* (Vol. 59, No. 3, May 2017), pp.73–80. For a more sceptical view, Jeffrey Bialos and Stuart Koehl, 'What America's Big New Defense Plan Gets Wrong', *National Interest*, 1 June 2016. See also Defence IQ Press, 'Russia Would "Overwhelm" NATO Land Forces', 5 May 2017; Gabriel Dominguez, 'DIA Chief Refers to China as "Near-Peer US Competitor"', *IHS Jane's Defence Weekly*, 31 May 2017.

18 Ray Alderman, 'Aircraft Carriers Are Just Big Fat Targets', 28 April 2017, <http://mil-embedded.com/guest-blogs/aircraft-carriers-are-just-big-fat-targets/ >, accessed 27 June 2017; Robert Farley, 'What Would it Really Take to Sink a Modern Aircraft Carrier?', *Foxtrot Alpha*, 22 April 2017, http://foxtrotalpha.jalopnik.com/what-it-would-really-take-to-sink-a-modern-aircraft-car-1794182843 accessed 27 June 2017.

19 Ministry of Defence, *Growing the Contribution of Defence to UK Prosperity: A Report for the Secretary of State for Defence* by Philip Dunne MP (London: MoD, 9 July 2018) p. 5.
20 www.adsgroup.org.uk accessed 14 December 2018.
21 MoD, Combat Air Strategy, 2018, p. 15.
22 Malcolm Davis, 'Technological change, future wars and the arms trade,' in Andrew T.H. Tan (Ed), *Research Handbook on the Arms Trade* (Cheltenham: Edward Elgar Publishing, 2020) p. 83.

9 'Partnering' and Defence Exports

Introduction

Notions around 'partnering' and the phenomenon's relationship with the defence enterprise are pretty well engrained now in current defence discourse and, often, equally baffling to practitioners and casual observers alike. The very modern narrative of defence partnering in the United King is rooted in the so-called Smart Procurement Initiative reforms, generated by the Labour Government's Strategic Defence Review of 1998. Derived from this, the MoD's Smart Acquisition Handbook of 2002 described partnering as the development and promise of a new, co-operative relationship between the British state and industry, with this relationship permeating national borders and commercial boundaries. The intention was to revolutionize and refresh fundamentally the commercial relationships and contracting mechanisms that would enable effective communications, the insertion of best-practice project management protocols and to build trust between MoD and industry. Consequently, this would supposedly minimize project threats and risks, uncertainties around contracting and generate the right defence capabilities to performance, schedule and budgetary targets and commitments. The MoD stated that[1]

> We have recognised that a partnering approach – building reliable links with industry – is often the best way of achieving the required performance ... The partner is given opportunities to achieve innovation and value for money.

From this early kernel of defence partnering, gleaned from organizational reforms and change management practices in the sunset years of the last century, partnering expanded to feature in international treaties, formal and ad hoc collaborations, the exporting of managerialist ideas from the United Kingdom to overseas' jurisdictions and, consequently, the replication of 'ways of working' that emerged in the United Kingdom to the territories of friendly or 'partnered' states. This allows the thought to percolate, perhaps, that the theories of partnering in defence, themselves, became tradable

DOI: 10.4324/9781003221494-9

economic goods, subject to commercialization by consultancies, advisory services and defence companies.[2]

This chapter considers these themes of partnering and the export of ideas, followed by a critique that challenges the credibility of such notions. The discussion begins, however, with an overview of the core principles of partnering, as they relate to the defence market, offering the reader an insight into the broader managerialist agenda of which the very narrative of partnering presents as an explicit and enduring component.

Principles of Partnering

Within this overall intention, we often encounter two terms; that of 'partnership' and that of 'partnering.' The Concise Oxford Dictionary describes a partnership as 'a state of being a partner, where partner is a person who shares or takes part with another, especially in business, with shared risks and profits.'[3] To partner, therefore, is to join with another to deliver a considered set of responses to requirements or system effects that are bounded and measurable. To put it another way, a partnership is a type of organizational practice that brings together two or more parties in order to achieve specific goals.[4] Typically, a legal agreement is usually in place when companies or customers-suppliers partner.

'Partnering' is a much more elastic term derived from the Japanese model of post-war engineering design and manufacture.[5] The organization that ultimately assembles and ships the product controls the relationship with its suppliers as a senior partner or 'parent' with component developers seen as 'children' to which the principal organization owes a duty of care within a long-term relationship. In this regard, specialist suppliers are recognized as critical to the overall quality of the product and essential to the brand.[6]

> There is recognition of expertise and quality running throughout the supply chain that binds customers to a prime contractor and, thereafter, to niche supplier, so that each is dependent upon the other, committed to this sense of quality, shared service goals and common expectations … . Critically, the specialist abilities of the sub-contractors are explicitly valued as crucial to the success of the overall product.

Thus, defence partnering is about a long-term non-adversarial strategic relationship between a government and a particular company or companies within the defence sector, with this arrangement being central to the delivery of effective and affordable capabilities.[7]

The Whole Force and Partnering

From its beginnings in the UK's Strategic Defence and Security Reviews of 2010 and 2015, the British Government and its armed forces have been championing something known as the 'Whole Force' as a way of promoting the, supposed, critical concepts of partnering in defence. This concept of the Whole Force was where military personnel, civil servants, reserve forces, contractors and multiple elements of commercial supply chains merged to develop, deliver and deliberately manage the capabilities necessary for the generation of sought-after military capabilities. This approach of 'enterprise management,' whereby the critical components and contributors of a specific output are actively managed and coagulate around collegiate common purpose, was intended to provide the route map and methodology by which the United Kingdom would generate its defence in the years ahead. Moreover, this concept of an active, holistic partnership between the public sector and private sector suppliers was eminently exportable as we shall determine in due course. The problem, of course, was that not all of the elements of the UK defence supply chain were properly understood or even mapped. Also, MoD personnel were not skilled in undertaking effective enterprise management as was necessary under a partnered approach. Rather, senior managers in government were invariably drawn from policy-making communities: it became clear that the philosophy of partnering was ill-matched by the skill set.

Partnering Between Companies and Government: The UK Training Estate

Nonetheless, companies across the defence sector, over the years, have come together to deliver goods and services to the United Kingdom through some kind of partnered model. For example, the Defence Training Estate has benefited from such a commercial solution. The Estate exists to provide secure venues, on a daily basis, to train military personnel to standards set by the individual Service chiefs, principally the head of the British Army. To do this, the Estate has to be managed economically and efficiently, with maintenance and enhancement of the natural and built environment as guiding principles. Complementing this, high standards of training itself, and broader environmental safety, remain ongoing, long-term imperatives, in turn, leading to the demand for effective management information and project management processes and practices. As a consequence, the competence set for the management and enhancement of the Training Estate is far from simplistic. Commercial businesses believe that if these management challenges can be satisfied in the United Kingdom, for the British Government, opportunities will exist inevitably for such solutions to be exported elsewhere, with such imperatives supported by the Government.

Indeed, the UK Government's involvement with such partnering concepts is central to the proposition. To respond to the complexity of organizational and managerial challenges across the Estate, military skills and public sector organizations and management principles have been blended with private sector skills and competencies to effectively manage UK military training. In this regard, Landmarc Support Services Ltd has been the incumbent managed services provider to the Training Estate, as administered by the Defence Infrastructure Organization (DIO). This company is a special-purpose joint venture, established in 2003, to provide support services to the DIO. The joint venture comprises Mitie, a leading facilities management and professional services company headquartered in the United Kingdom, and Amentum, a major provider of global mission services to the US Government.

Landmarc has close to 1,300 employees to provide safe, sustainable and effective military training across 120 facilities in the United Kingdom, representing a land mass of close to 190,000 hectares. Across this vast space, the main services provided to the DIO are the core management and operation of the training areas and ranges, coupled with built and rural estate management. To do this, a bespoke and sophisticated management information system has been developed. These elements are blended with core enablers such as catering and accommodation services, themselves running along with sustainable energy and waste management policies and practices.

In terms of the broader contribution of the partnership beyond these core tasks, Landmarc Support Services has generated significant economic benefits to the United Kingdom throughout its relationship with the DIO.[8] Annually, about £70 million is added in value to the national economy. Beyond this, the business has increased both the utilization of the Estate whilst, concurrently, generating additional revenues of £1.3 million. In terms of direct investment in the programme of managing the Estate, over £4 million per annum has been spent on direct savings measures and, significantly, £0.5 million and considerable staff hours were provided to create a fully digitalized asset management system and service to support, both, strategic decision-making and to enable the provision of effective management information for all stakeholders. The business has also invested in the development of career pathways for its own people and championed investment in a new institution called the Landmarc Academy to coordinate both the provision of qualifications and appropriate, career-developing experiences, as a single source of training excellence.

The defence training contract represents a complex, integrated suite of undertakings requiring the company to sit at the apex of a complex supply chain of environmental consultants, field officers, contractors focussed on land management services and catering and hospitality provision. As senior management within Landmarc Support Services has asserted[9]

> Landmarc has been partnering with the Ministry of Defence since 2003 … to ensure that the military training estates deliver a safe and sustainable place to train for our armed forces … Our ethic is to look for ways to create and add value in all aspects of our business activities.

This is significant, as innovation and reflective learning are critical to securing and maintaining enduring national advantage in the generation of defence capabilities. Quite often, though, the very idea of innovation is tied to emerging, niche technologies or new ways of exploiting existing knowledge. Seldom does it relate to training. Yet, in the field of defence, individual and combined force of arms and support training reside at the heart of the military experience and is proving to be a cornerstone of national security. Its strategic exploitation is essential to the health and wellbeing of the UK defence enterprise, ensuring operational harmony across the UK's armed forces and with allies, whilst helping to deter those who wish to challenge Britain and the West.

Training itself, therefore, and the implied innovation to its practice, is central to the generation of defence capabilities and successful defence outcomes and has been since antiquity. In the modern era, UK defence has utilized the Estate for the development and application of tactics and the teaching and learning of battlefield skills. In these regards, it is about the practice and honing of learning and the development of the effective mix of individual, team and team of teams' capabilities. It is difficult to think of many things more important than these to the effective practice of defence management. Given this, historically, the British armed forces, especially the British Army, have been well served by the Defence Training Estate: it is in the fabric of the military, recalled in enduring memories and reflections of training days.[10]

For a successful future, training requirements evolve to match perceived new dimensions of conflict. This embraces a wide range of situations in which military force might be used, from peace-keeping operations to major state-on-state all-out war undertaken, typically, as part of a formed or ad hoc alliance of nations. Consequently, those charged with training need to match the strategic resource of the Defence Training Estate to the ever-evolving characteristics of warfare. There is a dynamic relationship therefore between doctrine, training and capability that is not always appreciated by decision-makers, residing in the effectiveness of a commercial partnership. Moreover, it seems to be an established feature of UK defence doctrine that a range of interrelated factors determines the shape of conflict which, in turn, dictates required training policies and practices. These factors include things such as the nature of the participants; the degree of interest involved; the nature and extent of any limitations imposed; the character of forces engaged; the level of intensity; and, the actual or projected duration.[11] Add to these items, lessons derived from the so-called 'comprehensive approach' to interventions in Iraq and Afghanistan, then defence training, conceptually, as the critical component of capability, becomes a complicated undertaking to plan and administer.

Many analysts believe that the challenge for the next chapter of the Defence Training Estate, is the effective blend of successful and proven live training activities with exciting, though disruptive, emerging technologies. The private sector is well-placed to help with this, both in terms of early-year capital investment and the management of niche technologists within ever-changing supply chains.[12] Such a solution will prove, also, to be eminently exportable.

Exporting the Whole Force Partnering Model

As can be perceived, a company such as Landmarc has embraced the UK Government's themes of public–private partnering and played them back to decision-makers and end-users: this narrative is at the very heart of the company's operating model. This, in turn, has provided the template for exporting managed services to governments globally:[13]

> Building on [the UK] experience, Landmarc now offers a truly insightful, innovative consultancy and practical services supporting critical infrastructure and helping to deliver military and civil protection training across the world.

Specifically, Landmarc Gulf is registered with the Government in Abu Dhabi, United Arab Emirates, as a consultancy provider offering expertise related to facilities management; safety and risk management; training design and support; human resources management and environmental services. This offer to UAE officials and its military sits on the experiences gleaned from working in its home market in the United Kingdom. Without this, there could be no offering to other countries. This UK heritage and pedigree is the very reason why UAE decision-makers are attracted to companies such as Landmarc in the first place: the promise of a depth of experience with Western militaries coupled with this assertion, though vague and amorphous, of delivery through a 'partnered' experience. As Mark Neill, the managing director of Landmarc explains:[14]

> Landmarc Gulf reaches back into the capabilities and services of our family of companies in the UK and around the world. Our many years' experience directly delivering to the UK military allows us to provide a total service our Middle East export clients through Landmarc Gulf.

The centrality of UK operational and commercial experience to Landmarc's export solution to the Gulf region cannot be over-emphasized. This example stands as a vignette of a much wider reality for British businesses.

Commercial Partnering and Exports

As seen, a principal notion of partnering in the UK defence arena relates to this sense of the Whole Force approach to the subject – comprising the private sector, civil service and, of course, the military. This construct is exportable to other countries as a way of doing business, as witnessed through the Landmarc example. It is important also, though, to consider the potential for partnering between internationally focussed defence businesses, coming together to actively seek new markets and revenue streams. MBDA Missile Systems, for example, is a joint venture of three European defence and aerospace prime contractors, coming together to target the European and broader export markets in the design and production of missiles and their enabling systems. The UK-headquartered BAE Systems owns 37.5 percent of MBDA, Europe's Airbus a matching figure and the Italian-headquartered Leonardo the final 25 percent. From a UK perspective, being involved in this pan-UK-European joint venture allows BAE Systems a direct route to sales of such systems into European countries as well as offering an ability to subtly influence defence industrial and commercial policies in a number of European capitals.

In defence circles in the United Kingdom and Europe, MBDA is considered a rock star and the main model for partnered collaboration. Whilst some analysts regard the joint venture as essentially a UK–France–Germany–Italy commercial construct and pan-European defence procurement solution, providing complex weapons and materials to these nations, MBDA in fact has over 90 customers from around the world, working from offices, manufacturing and support facilities in these countries, but also from Spain and the United States. Based on 2021 commercial results, annual orders exceed €5.1 billion with a backlog in orders due to the COVIS crisis of about €18 billion. Revenues in 2021 were €4.2 billion. By any standard, it is a successful commercial entity contributing to the overall returns on investment of BAE Systems, Airbus and Leonardo.

Way beyond the abstract theology of the Whole Force partnering concept, and its derivatives, companies such as those in the MBDA joint venture come together to generate overt commercial returns such as those seen in 2021. But beyond this commercial success story, these businesses shape and come to define the defence operating environment they populate. MBDA's air-to-air and air-to-surface missile systems are in service with many of the world's modern air forces. For ground operations, MBDA has generated a product range of soldier-portable anti-armour and anti-air systems that are regularly seen in the world's conflict areas.[15]

Such weapon systems are critical in modern warfare as witnessed in the conflict in Ukraine in 2022. Post the Russian invasion in February of that year, the UK Government donated to the Ukraine forces over 3,000 next-generation light anti-tank weapon systems (NLAWS), manufactured not by MBDA but by Thales from their facilities in Northern Ireland. The weapon costs about £30,000 per unit and is fired from the shoulder of soldiers on the ground. It contains one armour-piercing shell that locks-onto the target vehicle to devastating effect:[16]

> When the invasion came, in February, the most crucial weapons were the NLAWS ... credited with knocking out many of the 164 Russian tanks destroyed, damaged or captured.

A selection of missile systems and counter-measures systems from MBDA, Thales and businesses such as Raytheon have played a significant role in the battle of Ukraine and moulded the manner in which urban operations can be conducted, potentially influencing significantly future military doctrinal choices. That such an effect can be generated by UK exports to allies, shaped by the narrative of partnering and the cold reality of dead-eyed commercial joint ventures, speaks volumes to the significance of these factors to the UK defence export story. Not unsurprisingly, there are other partnering concepts and narratives to explore as we can see next.

The UK–Australian Partnership – Type 26

After years of studies and discussions, the British 2010 Strategic Defence and Security Review announced the establishment of Type 26 (T.26) project for a ship to take the place of Type 23 (T.23) in the Royal Navy. With a weight of something over 6,000 tons, it was first conceived as an affordable warship to take the place of the T.23s built in the 1970s. It was to be a vessel that it was hoped would do well in export markets. Yet initial efforts to find export markets or collaborative partners floundered and the Royal Navy also increased the requirement specifications for the ship, taking it over 7,000 tons and increasing the expected unit price to about £1 billion, that is, broadly what the air defence T.45s had cost.[17] By the time a contract for the construction of the first three T.26 ships was signed by the Ministry of Defence with BAE Systems in 2017,[18] the Ministry had accepted that it could afford to buy only eight. Thus, to replace all the 13 T.23s in service, the Government, the Royal Navy and industry had to agree on a further, much less sophisticated platform, eventually designated the Type.31, of which six were to be built.

In June 2018, the Australian Government, after a formal competition, announced that it had chosen the BAE Systems' design of the T.26 frigate as the basis for its next-generation anti-submarine surface ship, known as the SEA 5000 Hunter class in Australia. For the UK, this was a success for a governmental and industrial marketing and sales effort dating back more than five years as well as a tribute to the expected range, quiet operation and other capabilities expected of the ship.[19] The Australian commitment was a unique event in that it was the first UK sale of a new major surface combatant in living memory. The T.26 was in fact so new that the production of the first ship was not then complete in the United Kingdom.

However, the Australian vessels were to differ from their UK cousins in significant respects: they were to be equipped with an air defence system including an Australian phased array radar, enhanced Standard and Sea Sparrow anti-air missiles from Raytheon in the United States, and the American Aegis Combat Management System with a Saab Australia interface. Responsibility for the physical construction of the ships was allocated to the BAE Systems subsidiary company in Australia.

Then, in October 2018, the Australia deal was followed by another when Canada, on a formal competitive basis, also selected the BAE Systems team and T.26 design for its next frigate.[20] However, the Canadian ship was also to be different from both the United Kingdom and Australian versions and Lockheed-Martin Canada was to build the ships at its Irving yard in Halifax, Nova Scotia.

Thus, from a BAE Systems and British government perspective, the T.26 design drove two successful export campaigns, configured as partnered solutions for respective nations.

There are many stakeholders for these partnered programmes in the United Kingdom, Australia, and Canada with different concerns and therefore different senses of what 'good' would look like. For the legislatures, the media and public, the financial weight of the three projects is a metric of significance that they can easily grasp and may well focus on. The sums involved are indeed large. The three Governments have different approaches to their release of costs, with the United Kingdom having contracted for initial and then more advanced work in increments. The Ministry of Defence eventually signed a production contract for the first three ships worth £3.7 billion in 2017.[21] Australia has specified the cost of its nine ships at A$35 billion although, as in the United Kingdom, a system of incremental contracting for individual steps and vessels is being used. Canada releases regular updated estimates to its parliament for the project cost including initial spares, and its latest estimates anticipate costs of C$69.9 billion, a much higher figure per ship than those planned in Australia and the United Kingdom.[22]

The British and Australian governments intend that these projects should make a significant contribution to regional and national prosperity through employment and the generation of skills and competencies, as discussed earlier in this work. In a closely related point, Australia and the United Kingdom also intend that these projects, in different ways, will lead to increased national defence exports, with Australia hoping that some of its sub-systems can be fitted in British ships. Finally, for the UK government, these projects are an outward and visible sign of global Britain in action in light of the decision to leave the European Union. They could and should facilitate wider operational and training cooperation between the two countries' navies and ease the way for more defence cooperation in general, including the use of Australian territory for test activities.[23]

The multiple objectives associated with the projects have two significant implications that need continuous attention and further exploration. The first, already indicated, is that there may well be no clear or uncontested metrics of programme success. The second is that the pursuit of multiple objectives almost invariable requires difficult prioritization choices. In the United Kingdom, there is established familiarity with the tension between acquiring rapid capability through buying a developed product off the shelf from an external supplier and a slower national development effort which provides home prosperity and national industrial capabilities. The Australian think tank ASPI has already noted that an early start to construction of the new frigates would boost employment but probably threaten cost estimates if detailed design preparations had not been completed.[24] A smooth ride for these projects in both states will require compatible prioritization choices by both governments and the companies involved. There is also the challenge of ensuring that one company, BAE Systems, and its complex supply chain work in a manner that optimizes the requirements and myriad ambitions of both national programmes. In many ways, that is a job for proactive programme management across the fleet build and through life.

AUKUS

The Type 26 experience taught respective governments and militaries in the United Kingdom and Australia that such partnered approaches to the generation of defence capabilities could be good for both the acquisition of military might and the export of materials and services to close partners. From such beginnings, major international security pacts are drawn. For example, a trilateral pact between Australia, the United Kingdom and the United States was announced on 15 September 2021, building upon the maritime work already undertaken by the British and the Australians, to help secure the Indo-Pacific region from Chinese ambition. The pact overtly focuses on military capabilities thereby separating it from the 'Five Eyes' intelligence-sharing alliance that includes the AUKUS countries along with New Zealand and Canada. The military capabilities in question are, specifically, cyber competencies, autonomy, artificial intelligence, electronic warfare, quantum technologies and the field of hypersonic research and defence applications. Specifically, though, the United States and the United Kingdom are committed through AUKUS to help Australia acquire nuclear-powered submarines.

The potential export of UK nuclear submarine technologies and competencies to the Australians are critical to its military intent and it is born of a long-standing commercial partnering narrative. Government alliances that are centred on information sharing and common standards come alive through the policy and management practices of defence exports. It could hardly be otherwise.

Conclusion

This chapter has outlined the philosophical journey from managerial notions of partnering to a construct of international allies and public–private commercial partners coming together to generate complex military pacts such as AUKUS. This narrative of 'partnering' allows the British to export ideas and concepts on how defence capabilities should be conceptualized and procured, as well as the materials, goods and services themselves. Thereby, the UK government exerts influence over partners whilst generating significant orders and returns on investment for its defence businesses. It is a sophisticated discourse with a hard-headed geopolitical and commercial set of purposes.

There is a reciprocal causation to this narrative: the circumstances of these partnered relationships and their influence over exports do much to shape these commercial and governmental constructs, but, conversely, the existence of these pacts and partnerships do much to determine their circumstances and execution. It is an elegant construct that has a logic and dynamic all of its own.

Notes

1 Ministry of Defence (MoD), *The Smart Acquisition Handbook* (Edition 5, 2004).
2 For a broader discussion on the migration of theory to an economic good, subject to trade and transaction, see Tony Tinker and Tony Puxty, *Policing Accounting Knowledge: The Market for Excuses Affair* (London: Paul Chapman Publishing Ltd, 1995).
3 *The Concise Oxford Dictionary, 8th Ed* (Oxford: Clarendon Press, 1991).
4 See, *The Gower Handbook of Management* (Aldershot: Gower, 1992).
5 See Richard Lamming, *Beyond Partnership* (London: Prentice Hall, 1993).
6 John Louth and Trevor Taylor, *British Defence in the 21st Century* (Abingdon: Routledge, 2019) p. 163.
7 See John Louth 'The Sum of its Parts: Partnering, the MoD and Industry,' in *The RUSI Journal*, April/May 2012, Vol 157, No. 2, pp. 6–11.
8 Social Enterprise UK and CAN Invest, *The Landmarc Difference: Report on Landmarc's Impact and Added Value in the UK FY2016/17* (Social Enterprise UK and Landmarc Support Services, 2018) pp. 3–4.
9 Social Enterprise UK and CAN Invest, *The Landmarc Difference: Report on Landmarc's Impact and Added Value in the UK FY2016/17* (Social Enterprise UK and Landmarc Support Services, 2018) p. 2.
10 Richard Dannett, *Boots on the Ground: Britain and her Army Since 1945* (London: Profile Books, 2016).
11 MoD, *British Defence Doctrine*, JWP 0–01 (London: CS(M)G, 1996).
12 Jeremy C. D. Smith Ed., *Defence Logistics* (London: Kogan Page, 2018).
13 www.landmarcsolutions.com [https://www.landmarcsolutions.com/about-us/who-are-we/landmarc-gulf] accessed 3 May 2022.
14 In conversation with the author in London on 10th march 2022.
15 MBDA has 45 missile systems and counter-measures systems deployed operationally around the world, combined with 15 next-generation programmes in research and development. See www.mbda-systems.com accessed 4 May 2022.
16 Tim Shipman, 'How Wallace fought 'securocrats' to donate UK's tank-busting weapons,' in *The Sunday Times*, 13 March 2022, p. 7.
17 It is difficult to specify a precise cost per ship, not least because the MoD contracted for the development work on an incremental basis. Additionally, the National Audit Office no longer publishes an annual report on the progress of major defence projects.
18 Ministry of Defence, *The Defence Equipment Plan 2018*, London, 18 March 2019, p. 23, https://assets.publishing.service.gov.uk/government/... data/ ... /20190318-EP18_v3.pdf
19 The British and Australian Governments signed a defence treaty addressing potential naval cooperation at the start of 2013, see 'Britain and Australia to work together to create possible frigates of the future,' 18 January 2013, https://www.royalnavy.mod.uk/news-and-latest-activity/news/2013/january/18/130118-uk-and-aus-type26

20 George Allison, 'UK wins Canadian Frigate Competition', 2 UK Defence Journal, 19 October 2018, https://ukdefencejournal.org.uk/type-26-frigate-wins-canadian-frigate-competition/

21 https://www.royalnavy.mod.uk/news-and-latest-activity/news/2017/july/02/170702-deal-for-t26-frigates

22 https://navaltoday.com/2019/06/24/canadas-surface-combatant-project-will-cost-c4–6b-per-ship-new-report-finds/

23 BAE Systems has already tested in Taranis prototype UAV in Australia and the British Zephyr High Altitude Pseudo-Satellite is also to be tested there, see 'High Altitude Pseudo-Satellite – soon to be undergoing testing by DE&S in Australian skies, *Desider,* March 2019, p. 22

24 A. Davies, M. Shoebridge and J. Mugg, *The Next Big Thing: Choosing Australia's Future Frigate* (Canberra: ASPI, May 2018).

10 Defence Exports and Military Cooperation

Introduction

Defence equipment and services exist to generate the military capabilities required by governments. The commanders of a nation's armed forces horizon-scan the equipment used by allies and potential enemies, identify what they like, and press their governments to develop or buy the desired equipment. In the case of British exports, the trade in arms is linked to British military doctrine, known ways of working across its armed forces, and cooperation and collaboration between militaries. If this is correct, understanding that doctrine is a key enabler of understanding defence exports from the United Kingdom.

This chapter, therefore, starts with a review of classic British military policy, bred from doctrine and the force posture generated as a consequence. It then goes on to discuss potential future ways of working and the impact changes in defence technologies and practices might have on future exports. The work concludes with a reflection on the change in UK military utility, from early 21st-century wars of choice to the peer-state competition envisioned for tomorrow.

British Defence Doctrine

Defence doctrine is described by the British as 'that which is taught' and the fundamental principles by which the commanders and planners of military forces guide their actions in support of political objectives. It is authoritative but requires judgement and nuance in application. In many ways, defence doctrine is the body of thought and hard-won lessons-learnt that underscores the development of defence policy, having its foundations in history whilst looking to future threats and risks, however hard they might be to conceptualize. As a consequence, for some analysts, British defence doctrine possesses more theological qualities than scientific:[1]

> Therefore, it is enduring, but it is not unchanging. Doctrine evolves in response to changes in the political or strategic background, in the light of experience or as a result of new technology. In turn, it influences the

DOI: 10.4324/9781003221494-10

way in which policy and plans are developed, forces are organised and trained, and equipment procured.

Doctrine, therefore, gives rise to three distinct requirements: an understanding of the levels of warfare defined as strategies; a set of guiding principles of conflict gleaned from this doctrinal belief system; and a structure in which to organize the military. As hinted above, the application of current and emerging technologies, and the manner in which they are procured and operated, influences all three intents. From the UK perspective, collaboration between militaries – across NATO, with the Americans and through AUKUS – is anchored in this sense of doctrine.

Strategy and the Levels of Warfare

There are four levels of warfare within British defence doctrine from which strategy is derived:

- Grand strategy: this is the application of national resources to achieve national policy objectives;
- Military strategy: naturally, this is the concentration and application of military resources to help in the achievement of those grand strategic objectives;
- The operational level is where commanders direct and manoeuvre military resources to achieve military strategic objectives; and
- The tactical level involves the direction of military resources to achieve cumulative operational objectives.

Taking the first Gulf War in 1991 as an example, Britain's grand strategic objective was, with allies, the removal of Iraqi forces from Kuwait and a return to the regional status quo. The application of the British military, collaborating with international colleagues, to conceptualize and plan joint operations to achieve this grand strategic aim was undertaken at the military strategic level. The Joint Coalition Headquarters and individual national headquarters executed the plan at the operational level whilst, within the coalition, the tactical level was the domain of various component commanders, such as the Royal Air Force Group Commander. The execution of doctrine in this manner allows all elements of a military force to cooperate and coordinate battle-winning capabilities.

The Principles of War

In addition, a number of military strategists and historians assert that the successful execution of military operations is dependent upon and influenced by a number of broad precepts that have come to be recognized as the Principles of War. These are as follows, acknowledging that[2]

The Ten Principles of War form part of the conceptual component of all military doctrine, informing the conduct of operations throughout the spectrum of conflict.

The Selection and Maintenance of the Aim

In war as a whole, selecting and defining the aim early, clearly and consistently. The purpose having been selected, it is fundamentally important that the application of force is matched to the required end state.

The Maintenance of Morale

High morale is possibly the single most important factor in long-term military success. Morale fosters the will to win, endure setbacks and sacrifice for a greater good beyond the individual.

Security

A degree of security through physical protection, stealth and information denial to the enemy is critical to the successful execution of all military operations.

Surprise

Surprise is a potent military weapon as it causes confusion and paralysis amongst enemy forces, sapping morale of the opposition's will to win. It is tied very closely to offensive action.

Offensive Action

Offensive action with targeted, controlled aggression is the chief method available to commanders to influence the outcome of a campaign or battle. It confers initiative to the attacker which is critical to military success.

Concentration of Force

Military success is normally associated with the concentration of force at a decisive time or place in the campaign. Agile assets that can be brought together quickly and decisively are highly desired.

Economy of Effort

The corollary of concentration of force and aggressive action is the economy of effort. There should be no wasted expenditure of effort where it cannot contribute progressively towards that decisive moment and place.

Flexibility

Although the aim should not alter, a commander should exercise nuance, judgement and flexibility of thought in its pursuit.

Co-operation

Military operations are joint enterprises involving cooperation between the services combined. The astute use of all arms in harmony, supporting and enabling each other, is important to effective operations.

Sustainability

This principle is concerned with the sustainment of a force on operations from force generation, through deployment and operations in theatre to recovery and recuperation thereafter. Without a focus on the sustainability of operations, a large element of the means to fight and win will be degraded.

From these principles, therefore, can be deduced the qualities required of the defence capabilities necessary for success – in the minds of the British, at least. Speed is a critical quality, as is the ability to manoeuvre and concentrate force effectively. Assets may need to be protected under armour, for instance, to operate and survive on the battlefield. From these principles and qualities come the armoured personnel carriers, tanks, helicopters, ships and aircraft that comprise the UK's order of battle. The line runs from strategy, through principles and defence qualities of the British military effort to the defence exports we see to friendly nations. Everything purchased by an overseas' government starts its journey rooted in the tundra of British defence doctrine.

That does not necessarily mean that the reader should believe the rhetoric offered by a review of British defence doctrine.[3]

> Despite military superiority, political strategic success has often eluded Western military efforts. It struggled to understand the character of contemporary wars.

The manner in which the military is organized might reveal some of this struggle and challenge.

The Organization of the Armed Forces

The British military order of battle is based on history and tradition. Since before the Second World War, there are three distinct branches of the armed forces in the United Kingdom: The Royal Navy, concerned with maritime operations; the British Army to undertake primarily land operations; and the Royal Air Force, for the undertaking of operations from, and in, the air. Reforming this structure into two branches of the armed forces or five organizations seems inconceivable. The Royal Navy has its own army element, of course, with the Royal Marines. The Army has traditionally its own air force with the Army Air Corps and the RAF has its own land forces with the RAF Regiment. To the outsider, it seems all a little confusing.

The historical benefits of organizing in this manner, though, are its simplicity, specialization and replicability. Commanders in the Second World War, for instance, thought that there were three operational domains through which acts of war could be conducted: on the land, through the sea (above and below) and in the air. Forming three forces to reflect these three domains was simple and logical. This logic, thereafter, allowed commanders and servicemen to specialize within a specific domain, with senior commanders only concerned with cooperation and coordination between forces within these domains. Where the British and other major military powers went, others could follow, so emerging and developing countries after the Second World War sought to replicate Britain's force structure by creating and populating an army, navy and air force.[4]

Saudi Arabia is a case in point. Seeking to populate an air force based on UK and Western doctrine, the Al Yamamah deal for 120 Tornado aircraft from the United Kingdom was signed in 1985. Seventy-two Typhoon aircrafts were then procured from Britain in 2007, with a memorandum of intent signed for 48 more in 2018. To arm these aircraft, 450 storm shadow missiles manufactured by MBDA in Stevenage, 1,000 brimstone missiles and 2,000 mistral portable missiles have been procured in recent years.[5] Without UK doctrine, historical force structure and ways of working, military forces in places like Saudi Arabia would not be configured in the manner they are. It is not an exaggeration to assert that a causal line runs from British military doctrine to British arms exports.

The Future Defence Environment

As introduced in Chapter 1, the British government's integrated review of defence, security, international development and foreign policy was produced in March 2021. It was promoted as the largest and most strategic review of the UK's defensive posture since the end of the Cold War.[6] As the guiding policy paper to take Britain into the 2030s and beyond, the visions for 'Global Britain' and 'Team UK' could be summarized as follows:

- The UK was poised to take a more active part in sustaining and protecting the international order in which democracies flourish, working collaboratively with friendly militaries from partner nations to protect human rights and international norms of trade and exchange;

- Prosperity would be championed through innovation in science and technologies that would both boost national income, British resilience and strategic advantage;
- As a maritime trading nation, the United Kingdom would champion free trade and commit forces to ensure that trading routes remain open and navigable;
- The main instruments of hard power, the armed forces and the intelligence and security agencies, along with the diplomatic service, would be transformed into the most effective and innovative organizations when compared to global peers, developing a critical national space programme and becoming one of the world's leading democratic cyber powers. New and emerging technologies would play a major role in enabling this intent.

The bulk of the UK's security focus would be on the Euro-Atlantic region, with NATO as the foundation of collective security in this geographical area. Russia was recognized as the biggest threat to the security of this region though, significantly, the policy review also talked of a tilt to the indo-pacific, conscious that by the 2030s, geopolitical and economic centres of gravity will have migrated significantly east of Europe. In this regard, China would continue to become increasingly assertive and powerful on the global stage, posing the biggest state-based threat to the UK's economic security. Accordingly, China-facing capabilities were to be invested in, including changes to the UK force structure focussed on the Indo-Pacific region.

It is significant to note that words such as 'prosperity' and 'economic security' were very much part of the fabric of a policy review focussed on defence and security strategy. Indeed, senior figures in government and the military were happy to brief privately that defence and dual-use exports, generated by the exploitation of emerging technologies and products, were a significant component of this thinking. This was overtly expressed in the DSIS, a companion document to the IR, again published in March 2021.[7]

Key elements of the DSIS comprised a commitment for at least £6.6 billion in Defence research and development funding and, in a reference to the report by Philip Dunne MP, committed the government to produce a new science and technology strategy.[8] There was a further commitment to draft a new small and medium-sized enterprise (SME) action plan to reinvigorate the relationship with smaller, supposedly more innovative design, technology and engineering businesses. Even more strategies were set to flow: a land sector strategy; an intellectual property strategy; a defence supply chain innovation strategy and a bespoke acquisition strategy for the newly formed Defence Centre for Artificial Intelligence. Moreover, the DSIS stated that there were to be a range of distinctive 'protected segments' of defence which were to be protected from overseas' ownership and interference.[9]

The guiding vision was for defence to be managed through a cat's cradle of emerging governmental policies and strategies linked not simply to a commitment to security but also to notions of prosperity, innovation, applied research and development and specific, sectorial reform.

Moreover, the IR pointed to the specific condition of the defence and security environment that is emerging this century. There is the sense that much of the next 30 years, or so, will be defined by traditional characteristics of great power competition, especially between the US, its allies and China, but played out across a profoundly transforming world:[10]

> For governments and militaries, the challenge will be in meeting the multiple dilemmas posed by different competitors: new proxies emerging quickly, geographically dispersed, quickly escalating and de-escalating, often planned to occur simultaneously.

The threats and risks posed by emerging great powers and their proxies will require a revolutionized tool-kit of fresh responses involving doctrines, ways of working, relationships and investment. But the critical change will be along the technological axis. Knowing about emerging technologies and their defence applications is proving challenging enough for any government or military. Thereafter, procuring and securing these technologies for the use of defence will bring their own difficulties.

A Word on Defence Acquisition in a Transforming Environment

This is where the practice of defence acquisition will prove critical. It is, though, a contested concept, frequently misunderstood and prone to lazy assertions rather than data-rich understandings. When *British Defence Doctrine*[11] was published in 1996, the conceptual base, moral base, personnel base, materiel base and infrastructure base were all lumped together as force enablers and little if any discussion was offered on technologies for defence, integration or the commercial acquisition of goods and services from an ever more sophisticated and disparate private sector. This was a little odd as a doctrinal assumption of the British, since the end of the Second World War, was that the nations of the United Kingdom would approach warfare, in harmony with allies (principally the United States) through a process of technological overmatch of adversaries. For NATO exercises and evaluations in the 1970s and 1980s, it was assumed that the Warsaw Pact brought mass numbers; the West, better technology. It seems a little silly for Defence leaders in 1996 not to be, at least, a little curious in regard to where these technologies came from or how they were to be generated in the future.

We know now, of course, that much of the technologies that underscore notions of Western military power are generated from the private sector and, significantly, are recognized as assets on commercial balance sheets, not government ledgers.[12] This matters a great deal to those who provide the capital. Accordingly, new methods of securing and accessing these disruptive technologies – processing and analytics, power-train solutions, digital modelling, artificial intelligence and advanced behavioural predictive algorithms, for example – are critical to the government, but such exquisite technologies developed through research, applied research, and development might not be offered to militaries for a notional profit margin of eight percent, or there about, as with British single-source regulations. Rather, with the most advanced disruptor technologies, owners want a return on capital in significant double figures at least. Government, and specifically the practices of Defence procurement, are not configured for such harsh commercial realities. Moreover, developers know that if technologies are transferred to militaries, outright ownership of intellectual property and commercial freedoms of action are diluted. Why bother, when more money can be made through the simple expedient of staying far away from the defence sector?

So, to manage this issue and risk, the British Government will need to invest more resources, overtly, in the early cycle of technology readiness levels (TRLs), in partnership with established and emerging businesses. This will need to occur if the British are to effectively collaborate with partner militaries in the future. Moreover, the government might have to hold an equity stake and associated voting rights to keep open opportunities as maturing technologies yield sought outcomes. As well as sometimes being wildly successful, investments in immature technology programmes often fail: the government will have to be content with paying for lessons being learnt, albeit sometimes in a painful and costly manner, rather than paying for technological certainty. It seems reasonable to assume that tomorrow's defence procurement portfolio might contain more incubating projects than classic, linear equipment-centric programmes. A whole new taxonomy of defence acquisition might have to be developed to deal with this rapid transformation in the art of capability generation.[13] The implications for the commercial function within MoD are significant.

The Future Operating Domain: Challenges for the Military

There are multiple trends associated with the future operating environment for defence assets[14] but they can probably be categorized under three distinct macro-issues. The first of these, as was briefly discussed, is great power competition for influence regionally as well as an emerging China–US rivalry for economic hegemony. Most aligned states and nations will be sucked-in to this competition which may often be presented as cultural clashes or values-based challenges. The competition will increasingly take place online through influence operations, misinformation campaigns and cyber threats. Geographically, the rivalry will be centred on the Indo-Pacific region.[15]

Second, the democratization of sophisticated intelligence, surveillance, reconnaissance and weapon complexes, along with their extended ranges, will mean that the West's notional technological advantage will degrade.

The case for British investment in innovative, disruptive next-generation technologies, as a consequence, will become increasingly compelling. The proliferation of these systems will allow states and proxies to create deliberate layers of control around their critical interests or areas of contention, denying access to their rivals – an evolution of the concept once known as Anti Access and Area Denial.[16] In discussion with the author, the then US Deputy Secretary of Defense, Robert Work,[17] outlined his thinking on the need to interdict capabilities that prevented Western forces from operating in their areas of choice. His view was that large, conventional forces were not survivable on tomorrow's battlefields – land, sea or in the air – and that democracies' decision-makers had to disaggregate their forces and favour smaller, flexible and sustainable units. Even these were going to have to seek sanctuary beyond the range of major guided weapons' systems or to hide within the 'bubbles' being penetrated. His view was that Britain's decision-makers had to re-seed the ground of technological advantage by turning to the suite of exquisite, disruptive technologies that were emerging and to marshal these technologies across a balanced and sustainable defence portfolio.[18]

The third distinct strategic issue is, of course, global climate change. The security aspects and imperatives of climate change, across society, are increasingly recognized. Militaries and their private sector partners must become more resilient and sustainable through policies and practices to mitigate the effects of climate change and to negate and neutralize great power challenges and asymmetric risks. There is synergy here, because the range of disruptive and transformational technologies necessary to compete militarily – at warfighting and below the threshold of war – given the first two trends, are the same technologies that should be used to interdict, slow down or reverse the effects of climate change. The defence enterprise's investment in the early TRLs of these technologies can serve both purposes to significant strategic effect. To plan for this, we need to see the Defence Enterprise, and the transformation strategies flowing from the IR and its associated policy papers, as a coherent portfolio of matured and maturing investments, required outputs and effects.

Defence in Transition: The Future of Military Exports

Over the past 50 years or so, we have seen from earlier chapters that British defence exports have typically been concerned with large maritime platforms (Australia) or multiple fighter jet orders (Saudi Arabia), as well as a plethora of small arms exports and dual-use enablers. We know, of course, that Team Tempest and the British government, for example, are basing the costing model for the development and operation of this aircraft on client-country adoptions and overseas sales. As we have seen from the preceding section, though, this century belongs to the technological innovator, not the bureaucrat, and we can expect defence systems to become increasingly complex, expensive to develop and (possibly) unaffordable to operate without significant collaboration between nations – Team Tempest is an excellent example.

This century might be one of transition, even revolution, in the sphere of military capability and what advanced (and aspiring) nations seek to hold in their armouries. This has profound implications for British policymakers as they seek export markets. The IR and DSIS both assume that British-registered companies are happy to be configured as constituent elements of a conceptual Team UK. Board directors may well be comfortable with the patriotic intent and benefit from the commercial branding but there will soon come a moment when owners and executives need to see the intended return on investment and the proposed commercial terms and conditions for any sale of long-term licensing of mature and emerging technologies. This will be the driver for commercial investment into research, applied research and development, not patriotism.[19]

Second, developments in additive manufacturing and sensor effects, for example, offer multi-sector employment possibilities for these technologies. Ever more innovative developments and enhancements will be focussed on non-military applications as there will be better returns for investors beyond the defence market. Defence ministries in the United Kingdom or within partner nations across the world need to work-through technology ownership models that mitigate the risks of technologies being trapped within a defence commercial vortex, denying the originators and owners the prize of commercial exploitation beyond defence systems.[20]

Third, artificially limited profit margins for single-source contracts may prove disastrous. Over the past decade or so in the United Kingdom, single-source regulations have capped profits on UK defence purchases to single digits, based on a cost-plus contract model. Very few exquisite, niche technologies will be made available to militaries for a profit of, say, eight percent, when inflation is running at 11 percent. Whilst data is scarce, some analysts and academics believe that target margins for Fast 3D printing, self-healing sensor networks and AI-based design and response solutions run at fifteen to 25 percent of direct costs, more if background or indirect costs are to be recovered. Defence contracts need to evolve to meet new realities.

Fourth, the narratives of the IR and DSIS, coupled with multiple commentaries since the launch of these documents, are ambiguous to the manner in which the UK government will fund the development of critical technologies as well as assisting on exports to target nations. This ambiguity is possibly borne from an over exuberance of expectation in what the government can achieve or direct. The Government has schemes such as the Defence and Security Accelerator which offers small upfront investments in the development of technologies at the lower levels of technology readiness, but it is a drop in the ocean compared to the private capital needed to progress technological development. Without a guaranteed sales pipeline, the large prime contractors are often stymied in their abilities to take a punt on a technology following governmental signalling of future requirements – the realities of shareholder and investor management makes such businesses risk averse. For agile SMEs, investor funds are critical often just for the provision of working capital and the promises of DSIS appear out of reach for many. Also, for companies not headquartered in the United Kingdom, but using the country as a staging post for exports, emerging British Government discussions around a refreshed defence offset policy might prove a disincentive to corporate engagement, as the loss of IP and transfer of production techniques to the United Kingdom may well be viewed as unattractive.[21]

Fifth, the vision of the United Kingdom as a high-tech armourer of nations forgets, perhaps, that the client nation still has a say in what it buys. Two thoughts are relevant here: partner nations over the years have been nurtured and 'parented' often by the United States – acquisition decisions for imports invariably have an American entanglement. Also, the defence procurement organizations of overseas' powers are often confusing and difficult to navigate for UK businesses, especially those with niche technologies new to the sector.

That is not to say that Team UK is fatally holed before it sails. But leaders and decision-makers need to understand these five core points and put in place mitigations to manage the risks they propose. One such mitigation could be to explore the role of the British Bank in a broad continuum of defence research and development funding and export working capital. Moreover, there could be 'stages of intent' triggering payments to industry rather than a full contract award being the sole point of commercial obligations from governments to industry. The UK Government could also take an ownership stake in companies most critical to the Team UK concept, especially those operating at the earlier stages of the TRL cycle. In this manner, the government would contribute to critical cashflows of, sometimes, fragile businesses and benefit from the rewards of ownership as sales mature. As the United Kingdom is no longer subject to European state-aid rules, a bespoke settlement for UK-registered businesses in support of government-stated strategic ambitions would seem sensible. In this regard, a flexible future offset strategy that understands the sweet spot between prosperity, technology transfer, exports and long-term commercial needs would assist corporate decision-makers.[22]

Conclusion

Military cooperation over the years has been derived from peer and client nations wishing to emulate the United Kingdom in how the latter generates military capabilities. To do this, countries such as Saudi Arabia have sought to access and operate British-generated technologies, integrated by UK-registered defence prime contractors into military assets such as advanced jet aircraft. Much of this requirement for such capabilities has been anchored in a desire to learn from and exploit the British military posture in regard to its doctrine and force structure.

The IR and DSIS extrapolated the importance of an effective and targeted military-commercial-industrial strategy to the objectives of UK defence and the country's contribution towards stability and security in the regions important to UK decision-makers: Europe and the North Atlantic, the Middle East and the Indo-Pacific. Military cooperation has been folded into strands of a complex, multi-component enterprise spanning nations, industrial sectors and technologies. Exports in arms from the United Kingdom, therefore, must be regarded in the context of this broader enterprise and range of British policy ambitions. Military cooperation remains important to this, but it is but one enabling component.

Notes

1 Ministry of Defence (MoD), *British Defence Doctrine (Joint Warfare Publication 0–01)* (London: MoD (CS(M)G, 1996) p. 2.
2 MoD, 1996, p. A.1
3 Frans Osinga, 'Strategic Underperformance: The West and three decades of war,' in Rob Johnson, Martijn Kitzen and Tim Sweijs (Eds), *The Conduct of War in the 21st Century: Kinetic, Connected and Synthetic* (Abingdon: OXON; Routledge, 2021) p. 17.
4 Charles Heyman, *The Armed Forces of the United Kingdom* (Barnsley: Pen and Sword Books Ltd, 2009).
5 Campaign Against the Arms Trade, 'Companies Supplying the War in Yemen' (London: CAAT, 2020) https://caat.org.uk/homepage/stop-arming-saudi-arabia/companies-supplying-the-war-in-yemen/
6 HM Government, *Global Britain in a competitive age: The Integrated Review of Security, Defence, Development and Foreign Policy* (London: HMSO CP 403, March 2021).
7 HM Government, *Defence and Security Industrial Strategy: A Strategic Approach to the UK's Defence and Security Industrial Sectors* (London: HMSO CP 410, March 2021).
8 Philip Dunne MP, *Growing the Contribution of Defence to UK Prosperity: A Report for the Secretary of State for Defence* (London: MoD, July 2018).
9 These are strategic nuclear capabilities, offensive cyber technologies, crypt key intelligence capabilities, complex weapons, novel weapons, test and evaluation capabilities, and chemical, biological, radiological, and nuclear protective and offensive capabilities.
10 John Louth and Peter Roberts, *The Victa Vision* (London: SSC, 2021).
11 MoD, 1996.
12 Trevor Taylor and John Louth, *The Challenge of Change: Acquiring Technologies for Defence in the UK* (London: RUSI Occasional Paper, March 2020).
13 For a discussion on state-led science and technology development for defence and industrial benefits, see Per Lundin, Niklas Stenlas, and Johan Gribbe (Eds), *Science for Welfare and Warfare: Technology and State Initiative in Cold War Sweden* (Sagamore Beach MA: Watson Publishing International, 2010).
14 See Michael Clarke, *The Challenge of Defending Britain* (Manchester: Manchester University Press, 2019).

15 See Bernard Jenkin (Ed), *Defence Acquisition for the Twenty-First Century* (London: Civitas, 2015).
16 See John Louth, Trevor Taylor and Andrew Tyler, *Defence Innovation and the UK: Responding to the Risks Identified by the US Third Offset Strategy* (London: RUSI Occasional Paper, July 2017).
17 Secretary Work speaking with the author on 2 December 2015.
18 See John Louth and Peter Roberts, *The Victa Vision* (London: SSC, 2021).
19 John Louth and Trevor Taylor, *British Defence in the 21st Century* (Abingdon, Oxon: Routledge, 2020) pp. 83–101.
20 Andrew T.H. Tan, 'Key Drivers of the Arms Trade,' in Andrew T.H. Tan (Ed), *Research Handbook on the Arms Trade* (Cheltenham: Edward Elgar Publishing, 2020) pp. 17–38.
21 Ministry of Defence (MoD), *Defence and Security Industrial Strategy: A Strategic Approach to the UK's Defence and Security Industrial Sectors*, CP 410 (London: The Stationery Office, 2021) p. 51.
22 See Ron Matthews and Jonata Anicetti, 'Offset in a Post-Brexit World,' in *The RUSI Journal*, 2021, No. 5, pp. 50–62.

11 Conclusion

On Reflection

This book began with a simple hypothesis: namely, that the subject of defence exports from the United Kingdom could be conceptualized through themes of geopolitics, prosperity, business, international development, national resilience, technological development, partnerships and military cooperation. All of these themes, however, at the outset were positioned to sit in the shadow cast by questions of ethics and morality.

What this exploration has revealed, perhaps, is that these themes cannot stand alone, but rather ooze into each other as the subject of arms exports proves to be amorphous and multi-dimensional. Whilst the nine themes of this enquiry allowed the subject to be accessed in the linear manner prescribed, only the subject seen in the round seems to offer a more profound understanding. In other words, a case clearly can be made for UK defence exports to be viewed through the lens of national prosperity, for example. But this has to be measured against very real ethical questions, themselves revealing untidy legal interventions by the government and complex constitutional questions. Whilst it was lawful for Prime Minister Blair to block investigations into exports to Saudi Arabia, for instance, on geopolitical, national security and prosperity grounds, was it ethically appropriate and the right thing to do? Also, political actions that enable corruption, protect the corrupt from criminal sanction and block the efforts of those attempting to exercise justice, themselves corrupt the British unwritten constitution. By any reasonable standard, such events provide a shock to our judicial system, quashes principles we seek to live by and erodes trust in political and commercial leaders. Given this, the price paid for UK defence exports is not merely financial, but reputational, as a bi-product of the exceptionalism of defence exports:[1]

> The arms trade occupies a unique place in international trade due to its key role [in maintaining] the monopoly of violence that is part of the very definition of a state. As such, it operates very close to the centres of political power in both supplier and recipient states, and operates under different rules to most other sectors, frequently in ways that enable corruption.

DOI: 10.4324/9781003221494-11

Region	% Exports (Based on £ values)
Middle East	58
Other	34
Asia Pacific	8

UK EXPORTS TO GLOBAL REGIONS: 2011-2020

Figure 11.1 Destination of Defence Exports.

Source: UK Government, Defence and Security Exports, 2020.

Also, it seems significant that the narrative of corruption, historically associated with these trade deals, originates within the undemocratic monarchies of the Middle East. The deals undertaken with Saudi Arabia, especially, are some of the largest the defence and security markets have ever seen. The Al Yamamah contracts of the late 20th century for combat aircraft and support continue to endure today. Between 2011 and 2020, the majority of UK defence exports, some 60 percent, went to the Middle East. In contrast, the nations of the Asia-Pacific region – an area of supposed strategic importance to the United Kingdom – represented less than ten percent of the materials exported (Figure 11.1).

Unquestionably, Britain is a major armourer of the Middle East and, if not the author of the recent conflicts in the region such as that in Yemen, must be viewed as a strategic enabler of the violence. This should make decision-makers in ministries and boardrooms uncomfortable (at the very least) when the bulk of recent exports from the United Kingdom to the region have their roots in the earlier questionable deals of Al Yamamah and its derivatives – the original sin of defence exports in the modern epoch colouring perceptions and understandings to the present day.

This poses a challenge for the UK defence sector, going forward. The policy posture of the government is to increase military and defence industrial interactions with the United States and Australia through AUKUS, building upon a successful maritime export campaign based on partnering and defence cooperation principles. In parallel, the United Kingdom is focussed on security in Europe, through NATO, to thwart Russian ambitions towards countries at the latter's western borders that were, in recent years, components of its Imperial and Soviet empires. We should expect more of the UK's defence exports to be going to Europe and Australia in pursuit of these policy imperatives, but the statistics point heavily to the dominance of the Middle East. If the numbers are reversed in the future, then the UK policy stance might be seen to be effective. Though, of course, it has to be noted that European peer-states possess defence sectors of their own that might limit UK penetration of these markets, especially post-Brexit. Moreover, countries like Germany, if it does recapitalize its military through increased defence spending, might prefer to use its Euros on US purchases as well as pan-European development programmes: the United Kingdom might be left out in the cold. As for Australia, once its own, on-shore, defence industrial sector is redeveloped and significantly expanded through initiatives such as AUKUS, the motivation for defence inputs from the United Kingdom, and future industrial collaboration, might be seen to wane. If this is correct, British dependence on defence exports to the Middle East might grow rather than slacken.

Michael Clarke was wise in arguing that UK defence has multiple futures not wholly defined and certainly not controlled by British policymakers.[2] The future the British end up with may well be much less than the option they would wish to choose. All that can be said with some confidence is that the export of arms, other lethal materials and their enablers, will continue as a joint venture of industry and state. The myriad reasons and rationales are contained within this book and the model introduced in Chapter 1 is reproduced in Figure 11.2.

For the activist of CAAT, the only question is an ethical one: a binary choice of good against evil. For this author, it is powerful and persuasive – in the heart, at least, if not in the head. For graduates of international relations studies, the dominant discourse and set of challenges revolve around questions of geopolitics. In contrast, the worker or family in Barrow might point to the criticality of national, local and familial prosperity and wellbeing. Businesses, themselves, will highlight the supposed realities of commerce and returns on investment in the real world of trade, opportunity costs and expensive sales campaigns. Markets and pricing mechanisms are imperfect, executives might say, but they indicate where investors should prioritize the pursuit of profits from the capital invested. The private sector goes where the customers with money happen to be, and surely always will do so.

Others might perceive that transactions that enable modern capabilities to be provided to the emerging world would have clear developmental benefits for client states, despite embedded challenges of corruption. For some, in

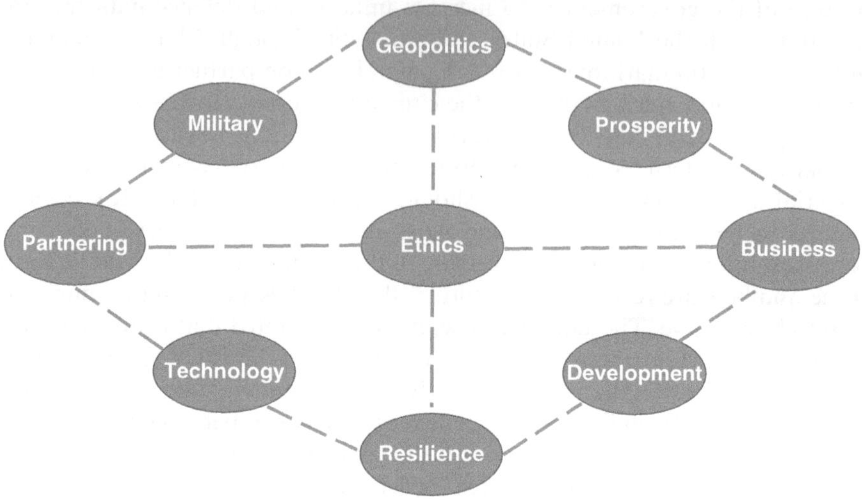

Figure 11.2 Multi-Perspective Model of Defence Exports.

Source: Author.

contrast, revenues from overseas for technology-rich defence assets keep healthy those firms that are able to generate such capabilities. This, in turn, promotes and elicits the UK's own resilience to shocks and strategic challenges. In this context, sharing in the financial fruits of technological development can only be a benefit of the exports in arms.

Themes of partnership and cooperation in defence also find champions though the realist never looks far from the money. In short, one can make a case for each of these approaches to UK defence exports, but none represents a definitive view. Rather, each perspective casts light and shade on the topic and on each other. For this author, that there are multiple arguments and contested ideas revolving around the exports of arms should hardly be a surprise. That these arguments should intensify as future defence capabilities become more expensive, technologically complex and, possibly, exclusive to smaller groups of nations pooling efforts to minimize costs, should also surprise nobody. For the companies involved in the defence sector, there are returns to be made, though significant financial, technological and integration risks to overcome. Regulators and politicians also will have to address more complexity and uncertainty as the sector and its trade practices evolve.

The model of understanding we have constructed, and the lessons gleaned through our journeys through UK defence exports, might prove to be of assistance with these endeavours. The components and themes of the multi-perspective model can be weighted based on governmental or commercial preferences, as we can see below. Competing investment options can be compared through the model allowing an evidenced-based conclusion to be constructed identifying the optimum investment to be made. Moreover, at a portfolio level, the model enables officials and industrialists to demonstrate that defence exports from the United Kingdom have been approved in a manner that addresses the main perspectives on a contested and controversial practice. For companies, this could also form part of their environmental, social, and governance (ESG) statements to markets and stakeholders, demonstrating the manner in which they have informed their decision-making.

Multiple-Perspective Model and Decision-Making

The model introduced in Chapter 1 can be formatted as a table with the perspectives weighted for importance based on the preference of the decision-maker (as in Table 11.1). This can be used to help businesses choose between which investments to undertake and for governments to decide on which exports to certify. It offers a simple and visible explanation to campaigners and citizens alike of decisions taken in terms of the application of exports licences whilst enabling administrations to 'weight' the importance they are placing on components of defence and security exports.

More sophisticated constructs of the Multiple-Perspective Model could be linked to costs of capital, discounted cashflows in investment appraisals, risk and opportunity management models, and other artefacts of portfolio, programme and project management practices. In this manner, decisions at the investment point and those taken at the point of export could be serviced by a common management tool, visible to all stakeholders.

Behind the headline number of such a model, narrative explanations of decision-making could be captured for each perspective, allowing governments to learn from early decision-making and focusing commerce on the key ingredients for export success. Its simplicity, and visibility, is the

Table 11.1 Indicative Multi-Perspective Model and Decision-Making

Perspective	*Weighted Scores Low-Left to High-Right*				
Ethics and Legal Considerations	0	5	10	15	20
Geopolitics	0	1	2	3	4
National Prosperity	0	3	6	9	12
Local Prosperity	0	2	4	6	8
Business Value	0	3	6	9	12
Development of Peer and Client States	0	1	2	3	4
National Resilience	0	3	6	9	12
Technology Development	0	2	4	6	8
International/Commercial Partnering	0	3	6	9	12
Military and Security Service Cooperation	0	2	4	6	8
Totals	**0**	**25**	**50**	**75**	**100**

Source: Author.

strength of the model with such a decision-making tool common to the Boardroom and Ministry currently missing from the UK defence industrial policy narrative.

The Challenge of Near-Future Technologies

The speed of technological advancement, its complexity, and the acceleration of technological redundancy all pose massive challenges to defence export markets this century. Defence analysts know that advancing technologies such as robotics, autonomous, networked and self-healing systems, artificial intelligence, directed energy weapons and hypersonic missiles are transforming the manner in which defence commanders and decision-makers across the sector are considering the critical components of future warfare.[3] It can be reasonably deduced, also, that emerging powers and client states in the Middle East, Asia, and beyond will want access to the latest Western defence systems and technologies as artefacts of 21st-century statehood and symbols of power. For example, advanced and complex fast jets, historically, have proliferated around the world, spreading their potential lethality as the user community itself has expanded. The next generation of these types of aircraft, such as that associated with the Tempest programme, are being developed in the United Kingdom and with partners with export potential very much at the heart of the business case for research, development and production. Without such exports, Tempest becomes probably unaffordable to the UK Government yet, with those exports, cutting-edge defence systems are proliferating globally. Moreover, whilst emerging powers are spending their monies on Western advanced defence systems, this is potentially at the expense of social programmes in their own homelands. As ever, ethical choices remain but now framed by the greater lethality and effective utility offered by a revolution in dual-use and defence technologies.

This notion of a military-technological revolution, underpinned by the IT transformation of the late 20th century, has led to some analysts to conclude that we are living through a moment of the so-called Revolution in Military Affairs (RMA).[4] This military-technological imperative promised for end users (and, importantly, purchasers) the prize of a critical and compelling military edge over known and potential adversaries. The ability and financial wherewithal to purchase and field such technologies yields, it is suggested, decisive military power even over the states in which specific technologies were incubated and developed. In a scenario where Saudi or Qatari spending power can secure an armoury of exquisite defence systems superior in range and numbers to that which the United Kingdom can afford to field, can UK defence exports continue as a transactional proposition? Yet without such commercial exploitation, the UK's ability to develop such systems for its own uses becomes ever more unaffordable. It is a wicked problem posed by the transformative nature of this century.

The lure of military superiority promised by notions of the RMA and its enabling, enhancing, speedily emerging transformative technologies should cause UK policymakers to pause, reflect ad perceive UK defence exports partially in the context of military balance and the UK's own national security imperatives. That such an approach could limit potentially future private sector investment in technological research and development would have to be acknowledged, and this in turn might have a set of negative impacts on policy ambitions for growth and prosperity. But the idea of the RMA suggests that states should think through the effects of offering their defence technologies to third parties through exports as mistakes could prove costly and strategically hard to rectify.

And Finally

The previous chapters have all hinted at uncertainty and a profound period of strategic shift in the century ahead. The one constant in the recent history of defence exports is the subject or recipient at the sharp end of the trade. We mean, of course, the deliberate or accidental (collateral?) target of the weapon system. Their fate remains the same and, in this principal regard, an exploration of the subject of defence exports will always be a matter of life or death.

Notes

1 Sam Perlo-Freman, 'Corruption in the Arms Trade,' in Andrew T.H. Tan (Ed), *Research Handbook on the Arms Trade* (Cheltenham: Edward Elgar Publishing, 2020) pp. 103–104.
2 Michael Clarke, *The Challenge of Defending Britain* (Manchester: Manchester University Press, 2019).
3 Michael T.Klare and Andrew T.H Tan, 'Emerging Technologies and the Arms Trade,' in Tan (Ed), *Research Handbook on the Arms Trade*, pp. 379–388.
4 Lawrence Freedman, *The Revolution in Strategic Affairs: Adelphi Paper No. 318* (London: International Institute of Strategic Studies, 1998).

Appendix – UK Defence Data and Statistics for Exports

Introduction

The UK Government releases annually national defence and security export performance statistics and analysis. The release focuses typically on single-year data but includes historical performance and outputs from other countries for international comparisons and also for purposes of trend analyses. UK defence export data is based upon returns provided by UK businesses following voluntary surveys conducted by UK Defence and Security Exports (UK DSE) or their contractors. International data is derived from open-source reporting of other countries' defence exports.

This appendix uses core 2020 data provided by UK DSE[1] so it represents the UK Government's own data in relation to defence exports. However, in the generation and utility of defence statistics, readers should always practice caution. There are myriad ways of generating a statistic set and, where data is generated by voluntary returns or contractors, the numbers might be the product of subjective selection. As academics have pointed-out previously:[2]

> An initial challenge in this area is that those collecting statistics on the value of defence exports vary in what they seek to measure and have access to different information that is, in one way or another, partial. Not surprisingly they come out with very different numbers.

The variables might be related to the value of goods ordered rather than those actually delivered, the difficulties of currency exchanges and the challenges of understanding and selecting just what should be included in the measurement of a defence export. For example, should the value of a company's offset investments into the purchasing country be included in defence statistics? On this point, there is no singular, agreed convention in the generation of defence statistics, leading many analysts to conclude that even supposedly national statistics generated by democratic governments should be treated as indicative rather than definitive.

As such, this appendix is comprised of a number of tables drawn from UK Government statistics as indicative of the state of UK defence exports.

Based on 2020 data and a rolling 10-year analysis, the UK Government asserts that the United Kingdom remains the second largest global defence exporter, after the United States. In 2020, the United Kingdom won defence orders worth £7.9 billion, compared with the previous year of £11 billion, perhaps illustrative of the volatile and variable nature of the global export market for defence. As a consequence, the UK share of the global defence export market was estimated at six percent in 2020. In contrast, the value of UK security exports was recorded at £7.95 billion, an increase from £7.2 billion in 2019. The challenge, of course, is that these definitions of 'defence' and 'security' are subjective with many officials and business people using them interchangeably. Nonetheless, it could be argued through such numbers that the UK's defence export market is shrinking whilst that of its security market is on the increase. The data below offer other insights and perceptions.

UK Defence Exports – Data and Statistics

The following tables are provided to illuminate the UK's efforts relating to exports of defence and security materials and services (Table 1).

Table 1 UK and International Defence Export Market Share (2020, %)

Country	*%*
USA	68
Russia	9
UK	6
France	3
Italy	1
Germany	1
Others	12

Source: UK DSE.

Table 2 Defence Export Market Share – 10 Year Trend to 2020 (%)

	2011	*2012*	*2013*	*2014*	*2015*	*2016*	*2017*	*2018*	*2019*	*2020*
USA	35	48	36	39	43	40	52	40	47	68
Russia	14	10	11	9	10	12	17	13	11	9
UK	15	16	22	15	11	9	13	19	17	6
France	13	7	9	8	18	12	7	9	10	3
Italy	4	2	1	1	1	9	1	2	2	1
Germany	5	2	9	3	2	4	3	2	2	1

Source: UK DSE.

Table 3 UK Exports to Global Regions – 10 Year Trend to 2020 (%)

Global Region	%
Middle East	58
North America	17
Europe	15
Asia-Pacific	8
Africa	1
Latin America	1

Source: UK DSE.

Table 4 Top-Ten Nations for Defence Exporters Based on Contracts Awarded – 10 Year Trend to 2020 ($ billion)

Country	*$ Billion*
USA	445
UK	125
Russia	108
France	85
Germany	30
Spain	25
Italy	25
Israel	20
Canada	18
Sweden	15
Total	896

Source: UK DSE.

Table 5 Top-Ten Nations for Defence Imports Based on Contracts Awarded – 10 Year Trend to 2020 ($ billion)

Country	*$ Billion*
Saudi Arabia	120
India	59
Qatar	58
Australia	57
USA	28
Egypt	23
UAE	22
Canada	19
Kuwait	18
UK	17

Source: UK DSE.

Table 6 Defence Export Market by Sector Based on Contracts Awarded – 10 Year Trend to 2020 (%)

	Aerospace/Air Systems	*Land Systems*	*Maritime*
Global %	65	22	13
UK %	91	5	4

Source: UK DSE.

Table 7 UK Security Export Market by Sector Based on Contracts Awarded – 5 Year Trend to 2020 (£ Billion)

2016	*2017*	*2018*	*2019*	*2020*
4.2	4.8	5.2	7.1	7.9

Source: UK DSE.

Table 8 British Security Exports' Destination by Region in 2020 (%)

Region	*%*
Europe	44
North America	27
Asia Pacific	14
Middle East	8
Africa	5
Latin America	2

Source: UK DSE.

Table 9 British Security Exports by Materials in 2020 (£ Million)

Materials	*£ Million*
Cyber Security	4,231
Screening and Detection Equipment	1,077
Fire Equipment	589
Data Analytics	378
Surveillance Materials	375
Access Control and Identity	341
Communications Equipment	341
Managed Services	177
Platforms and Vehicles	128
Risk Management Services	107
Personal Protection Gear	104
Command and Control Equipment	81
Disaster Management Services	19

Source: UK DSE.

Table 10 Global Security Exports by Country in 2020 ($ Billion)

Country	*$ Billion*
USA	19
China	12
UK	11
Germany	9
France	6
Hong Kong	5
South Korea	5
Italy	3
Japan	3
Canada	3
Total	76

Source: UK DSE.

The obvious point to make is that the United States has, by a significant margin, the highest percentage share of the market, with its European competitors lagging significantly behind. A number of US exports have, of course, gone to their European allies suggesting, for some, that the European powers are defence clients of the Americans. It seems significant, also, that an emerging global power, such as China, seems unworthy of tracking in UK defence statistics and, from a UK DSE perspective, we can only wonder at how much of the remaining 12 percent of the defence exports market falls to China. It might be, of course, that China has been focused on its own recapitalization of its armed forces and is deliberately absent from the defence exports' market. The point is, the UK national statistics are silent on this point leaving analysts to seek other data sources. Moreover, that Russia, with an economy roughly the size of that of Italy, can secure almost ten percent of the global market, seems remarkable and points towards Russia's continuing geopolitical significance.

This is an interesting trend analysis. At the beginning of the decade the United States, whilst dominant, was matched and exceeded by combined European sales, hinting at a much more pluralistic market. By the end of the decade, the US defence sales far exceeded those of the Europeans by almost six to one. In terms of defence exports' sales, the United States had evolved into the hegemon. The United Kingdom, in contrast, appeared to be in decline by 2020, significantly reduced from the double-digit percentage market share of the preceding decade.

The key element of this table is that defence sales to the Middle East over this period significantly dwarfs other transactions. This is interesting in that UK defence doctrine focuses on European mainland defence through NATO and support to the US-led world order in challenging Chinese geopolitical ambitions, mostly in the Asian-pacific area and the South China Sea.

Yet, UK defence export commercial activity is focussed not principally on these geographical areas but on the autocratic monarchies of the Middle East. Whilst motivations around the generation of allies and, thereafter, their development and security, is complicated and nuanced, there is at least a thought that defence exports from the United Kingdom have followed the money not necessarily the UK's geostrategic interests. For those who draw such a conclusion, this table could offer a statistic set in support of such an argument.

Over the ten years to 2020, US exports represent, in effect, half of the global market that, over that period, equates to approximately $0.9 trillion. This is a massive market and, whilst the United Kingdom comes in second in the table on sales, the country's decline in 2020, relative to rivals, reveals an impactful shrinkage of a significant global sector for exports. Should this trend continue, the UK's geopolitical standing and the country's policies around prosperity through defence exports could be significantly impacted.

It seems significant that the powers of the Middle East should feature so heavily in a table of defence importers, suggesting that the United Kingdom has followed the money. Whilst there are multiple explanations for the UK–Saudi Arabian relationship over this period, it is hard not to conclude that motivations around commerce and income generation form part of the narrative. The UK Government and business executives from defence companies located in the United Kingdom have concluded that export campaigns should be focused on countries with a policy need for the acquisition of defence systems and a willingness and ability to pay. Some analysts might conclude that geopolitical considerations have, perhaps, followed this commercial reality with discourses around alliances and development being used to legitimize sales. Also significant is the United Kingdom, itself, being revealed as the tenth-largest importer of defence systems and materials over a rolling ten-year period. This suggests that the UK's on-shore defence industrial base cannot furnish the British Government with all of its defence material needs and also hints, arguably, at the international nature of defence industrial actors and supply chains.

This table suggests that the international defence market, in recent years, should be conceptualized as predominantly an aerospace export market, based on value. Aircraft are typically at the cutting edge of available defence technologies, expensive and ordered in multiples typically with maintenance solutions included so, perhaps, this should not be too much of a surprise. Also, the main importers, such as Saudi Arabia, appear to prefer artefacts of military modernity – fast jets very much suggest advanced military prowess. Within this context, the UK's experience of defence exports is very much an aerospace story. Over 90 percent of exports relate to the air sector, and commitments to the F35 programme and the UK Tempest programme suggest that aerospace exports will remain significant to the United Kingdom well into the next three decades. However, the extant political narrative around the maritime Type 26 programme, Type 31 and the geopolitical pivot to the Asia-Pacific area all point to a renewed ambition for maritime exports. The historical data suggests that the poor cousin remains land military systems with questionable commitments to Army future requirements and a paucity of export opportunities given a hollowed-out land systems industrial base. This seems strange given that the experience of Ukraine, which the United Kingdom is committed to learn from, is in essence a narrative of land warfare and the physical occupation of contested real estate. That there is a near-future requirement for land systems seems obvious but, on historical trends, the UK's focus has been unwavering in its support for aerospace development and exports.

Whilst there is no strict division between 'defence' materials and 'security' equipment, the convention across governments is that the former is concerned with capabilities that are used by militaries – typically, aircraft, ships and armoured personnel carriers, for instance – whilst security items are usually those used by the police, security services or homeland militias. Such items include cyber security protections, detection equipment, communication capabilities and personnel protection equipment. Data for security exports is less complete and usually generated by private companies working under contract for the British Government.[3] In each of the five years for which data was generated, security export materials increased as a trend between 10 percent and 37 percent in the previous year. Given this, it seems sensible for the British Government to focus on a Defence and Security Industrial Strategy, as security exports seem a growth area.

In terms of security exports, the principal destinations are the democracies of Europe and North America – reassuring for some analysts and campaigners given the potential for the repressive use of some security sector materials. Less comfortable for some, perhaps, is the sale of materials to the autocracies of the Middle East, mirroring the UK's commitment to the region through parallel and historical defence exports.

Mindful that over 70 percent of the security export market from the United Kingdom is targeted in Europe and North America, it seems remarkable that the United States, France, and others are importing from Britain, cyber security services, screening and detection capabilities and fire services and equipment. An assumption, without access to the data, would be that such democracies would generate such capabilities and competencies from their home markets, favouring home-grown companies as part of commitments to respective national resilience policies. That the United Kingdom is growing in such sectors suggests global expertise, especially in cyber security, exports of which have grown year-on-year since 2016, almost tripling in output over the five-year period. Of interest, over the same period, much of the market for personal surveillance, UK exports of which are fast approaching £0.5 billion, are centred on countries in the Middle East.

This data set is interesting as it shows China taking a leading role in the security exports market, second only to the United States. This is in direct contrast to its near-ghost presence in the defence exports market. If the exports from Hong Kong are included, which are recorded under the supposed 'one country, two systems' construct for China, security exports would be almost on a par with the Americans. This hints at the Chinese policy orthodoxy of investing in and providing services to a state's core national infrastructure and represents a security challenge to the Western democracies. In terms of the United Kingdom and the security export market, Britain has a solid and growing presence in the market, currently coming in third behind the United States and China.

Conclusion

The data contained in these ten tables suggest that the defence market is contested, complicated and nuanced. The United Kingdom has performed well historically, especially in the exports of aerospace/aircraft systems but now appears to be in gentle decline. The importance of F35 exports and the development of Tempest as an exportable platform cannot be understated. In terms of security, a much smaller export market than that of defence, but the United Kingdom is performing well, especially in the exports of cyber security equipment and services which dominate the sector. Such statistical insights should inform UK defence and industrial

Policy in the coming decade and beyond.

Notes

1 https://www.gov.uk/government/statistics/uk-defence-and-security-exports-for-2020/uk-defence-and-security-exports-statistics-for-2020
2 John Louth and Trevor Taylor, *British Defence in the 21st Century* (Abingdon, OXON: Routledge, 2019) p. 106.
3 In the five-year data sample reviewed, Frost and Sullivan provided four years' worth of statistics whilst Westlands Advisory generated data for 2018.

Index

Note: **Bold** page numbers refer to tables and *italic* page numbers refer to figures. Page numbers followed by n and number represent endnote and note number respectively.

For Product Safety Concerns and Information please contact our EU representative GPSR@taylorandfrancis.com Taylor & Francis Verlag GmbH, Kaufingerstraße 24, 80331 München, Germany